CUT, FOLD & HOLD

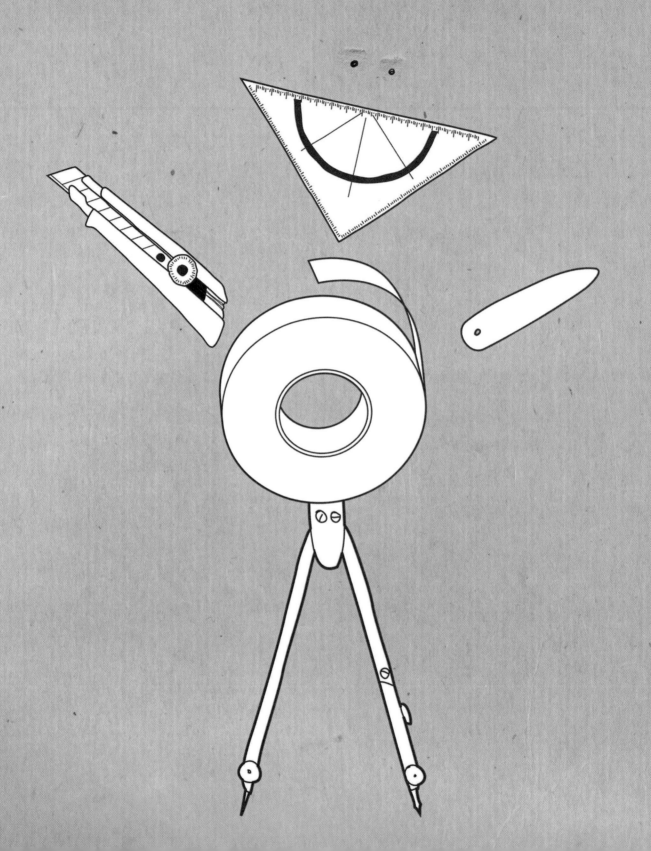

SOSUMI

CUT, FOLD & HOLD

Unique Cardboard Projects for the Home

HELLO... WE ARE SOSUMI

Sosumi? Yep! Our names are Petra and Dirk, we're from Frankfurt am Main and we run a design office called just that—Sosumi! What do we do? Well, of course "office" sounds like an awful lot of paper shuffling and computer work, with everything flat as a computer monitor and as dull and empty as a blank sheet of paper. But Sosumi wouldn't be Sosumi if we had been satisfied with two dimensions—we had to have one more! Come with us to the third dimension, where everything is a little more thrilling, a little more evocative and a lot more exciting to touch...

THIS OFFICE stray represents our quest for the third dimension. Bored with the two dimensions of its cardboard existence, it folds itself into a new shape and prowls the office, leaving no desk or meeting room safe.

www.sosumi.de

WHAT INSPIRED THIS BOOK?

The basic idea came, as is often the case, from everyday life. Almost everyone has had that moment when the penny drops. Imagine this scenario:

You buy a new desk from the furniture store that you have to assemble yourself.

You're ecstatic when it's finally put together...

...but you have an enormous pile of packaging material to get rid of. This is mostly corrugated cardboard, and it fills almost half of a recycling bin.

Sound familiar? Turn the page!

Most of the time there's nothing wrong with this beautiful cardboard; it's new, smooth, sturdy and simply a shame to throw away.

WHY IT'S A SHAME TO THROW AWAY CARDBOARD:

Why throw something away when you could create beautiful crafts with it? We love this material, and corrugated cardboard in particular. Corrugated cardboard is the Space-Age super-stuff of all available craft materials. What's that? We exaggerate, you say? Pay attention, then:

Although cardboard is made of lightweight, thin, recycled paper, it is impressively strong and extremely flexible to use.

CARDBOARD is one of the most sustainable materials a person can use. Keep in mind the words "recycled paper." The material has already been created from old paper, and the cardboard that you use will surely have already been used for packaging or another similar purpose; as such, it's contemptuously called "waste."

CARDBOARD is warm and appealing to the touch; the surface is smooth and attractive.

CARDBOARD is constantly available in a variety of thicknesses. If during construction you find that you're missing a piece, as a last resort you'll be able to find what you need in your neighbor's recycling bin. There's no need for laborious hunting for expensive specialized materials!

CARDBOARD from recycling bins and other similar sources is free. A high-tech material for free—where else can you get this? Cardboard can be found everywhere and is always available; why would anyone ever pay for it?

CARDBOARD can be brilliantly crafted with the simplest of hand tools, and it lends itself to a variety of finishing methods.

CARDBOARD saves time! Because of the simplicity of processing cardboard and its high availability, it's great for experimentation or just testing out ideas. It's crazy when you consider how quickly you can try out a project with cardboard—just lay it out, draw out the plan, cut it out, glue it together and you're done. A functionality test needs no more than five or ten minutes, and if it doesn't work, just start over. Cardboard is great for learning by doing!

CARDBOARD has a natural appearance, and, when used with beige or brown kraft tape, takes on a very high quality finish that looks almost like wood.

CARDBOARD is a material that can be used to build almost anything. You'll be amazed at how sturdy some of the constructions in this book are! If you search the internet you can find people constructing entire rooms, emergency shelters, functioning bikes, boats and more out of cardboard.

ALL IN ALL, CARDBOARD IS AN IDEAL BUILDING MATERIAL!

ABOUT THIS BOOK:

This is a book about the basics of working with cardboard. In contrast with most DIY instructions, we will show you exactly how, with very little expense, you can design and build your own projects, much like you would in a woodworking workshop. But you don't need a workshop—these projects can be built in your own home!

We've developed a method for the projects that is easy to follow and will yield satisfactory results, even for beginners. Because it is difficult to precisely fold corrugated cardboard at home, every project uses individually cut pieces bound together with kraft tape. This way you are always in control, and the finished projects are precisely built. This method not only ensures high-quality work, but bestows the trustworthiness of the planned design, accurate handiwork, and carefully implemented features to your cardboard work.

In "Cut, Fold & Hold," you will find a wealth of basic knowledge for working with cardboard and other materials. Here you will find important details about building materials, different tools, and adhesive, as well as detailed instructions for the various projects.

It was very important to us when planning this book that even the basic techniques be explained. For example, we've always wanted a book that clearly explained what to look for in a craft knife and the best techniques for handling one. There are a number of simple but incredibly helpful tricks for using a craft knife—one just has to know what they are! We're certain that these instructions will not only help you with our projects, but also any future ones you take on.

Don't take our 35 projects as a definitive guide, but as a base of craft techniques you can build on. This base can be updated and expanded as needed to achieve the best results.

Each of us has had a crooked corner in our home, or a gap at the end of a shelf with odd measurements.

With this book we hope to inspire your creativity and provide techniques that will enable you to develop your own solutions to the tricky problems that may arise in your own home. We think you'll love no longer being dependent on store-bought objects and instead being able to design and construct your own functional, unique objects.

Finally, some words of wisdom: don't be scared to make mistakes! Cardboard is made of paper, which we all know is very forgiving. Working with cardboard is often such a fast process that it's no big deal to rebuild some elements if something goes wrong. And because the projects are constructed with kraft tape, you will often only need to cut once or twice to take pieces apart. It's only through trial and error that we're able to learn; as the saying goes, "practice makes perfect!"

Good luck and have fun!

PETRA SCHRÖDER & DIRK VON MANTEUFFEL

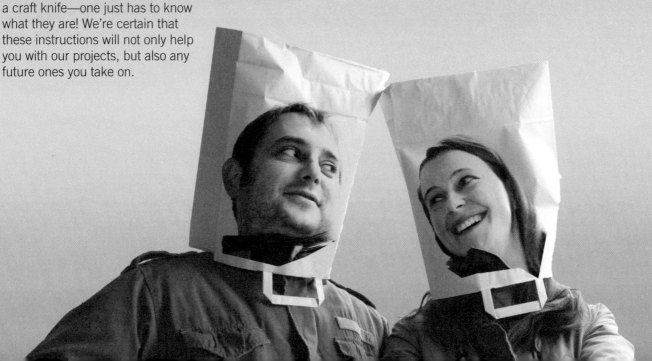

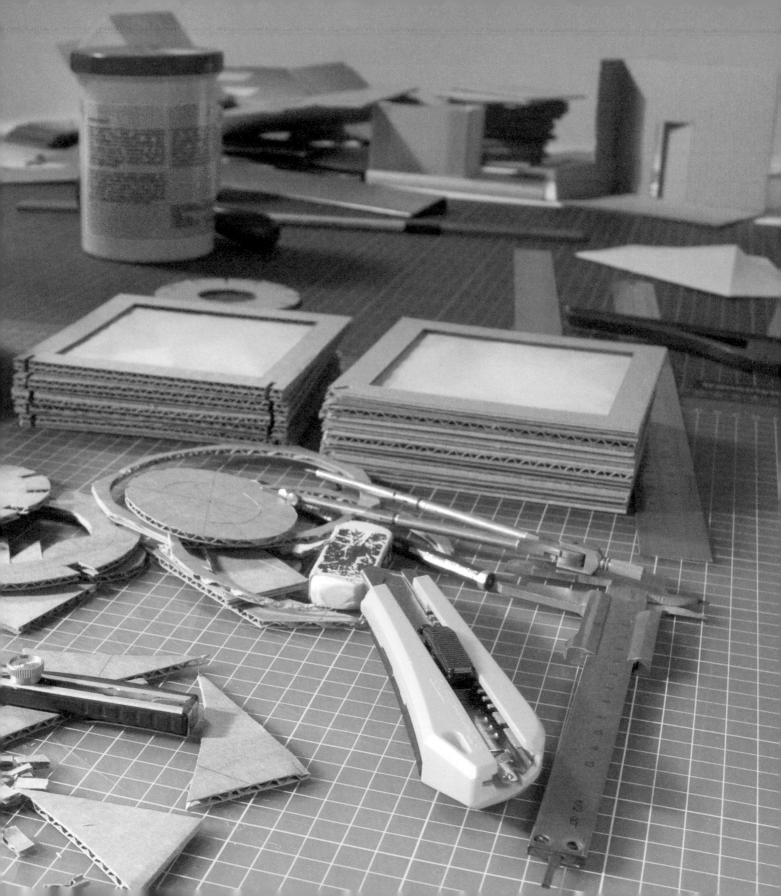

CHAPTER 1

BASICS

CARDBOARD

Conserving Resources:

Cardboard, in particular corrugated cardboard, is the material of choice for the projects in this book. The reason we like using this material is as simple as cardboard itself; it can be handled with the simplest of tools, it can be glued and painted, it is available everywhere in all kinds of variations, and it usually costs nothing. In addition, cardboard is often only used once as a packing material and then thrown away... what a waste!

In fact, we use waste material for our work. This is good for us because it costs nothing, and good for the environment because it reduces waste. If we look even more closely, we're using waste from material that has already been recycled—namely, recycled paper! It's twice as good when recycled materials are put to use again. The best thing, though, is that an object built from three different printed boxes doesn't require any further finishing. Cleverly selected prints are decoration enough.

Two kinds of cardboard are used for these projects:

Greyboard:

Greyboard is a homogeneous material which can be found in thicknesses of 0.5mm and up. It can usually be found in food packaging with a thicknesses between 0.5-1mm (cereal boxes, frozen pizza packaging, etc.). Sturdier boxes are made of a material with a thickness of 4-5mm. If you want to bend greyboard, you have to take note of the direction of the grain.

Greyboard is more pliable when bent perpendicularly to the direction of the grain than parallel to direction of the grain. You can test it simply by trying to bend it in both directions.

Corrugated cardboard:

Smooth and corrugated paper rolls are glued together to produce corrugated cardboard. The resulting material is light, easy to treat and work with, and incredibly sturdy. Cardboard with a thickness of 1-6mm has been used for the instructions in this book. The difference in quality of corrugated cardboard can vary greatly. You'll know when you first hold it whether it's a suitable craft material or not. High quality cardboard, even in thinner thicknesses, is resilient under pressure and feels stiff and smooth. You can rely on your hands to tell you whether a piece of corrugated cardboard is good quality or not. We come across this material everywhere: product packaging, furniture packaging and moving boxes are some of the main sources of this material.

GREYBOARD (0.5mm)
Food packaging (for example, cereal boxes),
electrical appliances, tabloid-size and larger
padded envelopes.

GREYBOARD (1mm)

CORRUGATED CARDBOARD (1mm)
light packaging

CORRUGATED CARDBOARD (2.5mm)
furniture packaging

DOUBLE CORRUGATED CARDBOARD (4mm)

CORRUGATED CARDBOARD (4mm)
Undamaged cartons from the
supermarket

DOUBLE CORRUGATED CARDBOARD (6mm)
Packing boxes, large, sturdy boxes
for fridges, furniture, etc.

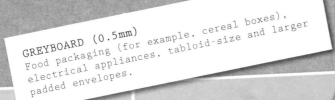

TIP

All cardboard and cartons have
two sides, a front and a back.
Greyboard is smoother on the
front; the back has a much rougher
texture. The covering layer on the
back of corrugated cardboard is
often thinner and wavier than
the front.

PAPER

Telling stories:

Even if paper is only used for finishing and decoration in this book, it's still an important and useful medium that goes beyond the material itself. Paper can tell stories. Freshly unpacked printer paper can't do this yet, but other paper can: old maps, flyers, posters, used wrapping paper, tickets, comic strips, newspapers and magazines, even printed paper and other found scraps have stories to tell. These stories can be horrifying, factual, autobiographical, nostalgic or out-of-this-world, depending on the paper used.

All paper can be used in pleasing and functional ways! For neutral surfaces one can let the material speak for itself, or cover it with Nepalese paper, thick, handmade paper, or attractive wrapping paper.

Paper is multi-layered.

WHAT EXACTLY IS PAPER WEIGHT?

The "paper weight" refers to the weight of one ream of paper. Ordinary copier paper usually has a paper weight of 20 pounds, which means that 500 sheets weigh 20 pounds. This surface density allows us to compare different qualities of paper.

COMMON PAPER WEIGHTS ARE:

Newspaper   16lb
Copier paper   20lb
Packaging paper   40lb
Flyer card paper   66lb

With paper weights of approximately 100 to 400 pounds, we're talking about cartons; at a weight of 400 pounds we're talking about cardboard. When the weight is over 650 pounds the material thickness is also specified.

PACKAGING

Get Inspired:

Carton packaging is one of our main sources of craft material. Not only are cardboard cartons versatile and readily available, they often already have elements or features that can be reused or converted for your use. Folds in the material, (reinforced) holes, inserts and other features are particularly useful.

If you look at the magazine file box (p. 106), you will see that the front corners are folded. Normally we would put something like this together from separate pieces of material to ensure it's as precise as possible. However, for this we reused packaging material that already had the right dimensions for the project. Why build it from scratch when you can save yourself a few steps?

A great source for large quantities of cardboard is furniture packaging. The kind of corrugated cardboard used for this is often very thin and sturdy, making it ideal for our projects.

Instead of decorating your objects after they're done, you might want to work with cardboard that matches the other pieces in your project, or has already been printed on. Fruit bags often have beautiful prints, as do cartons from Asian markets.

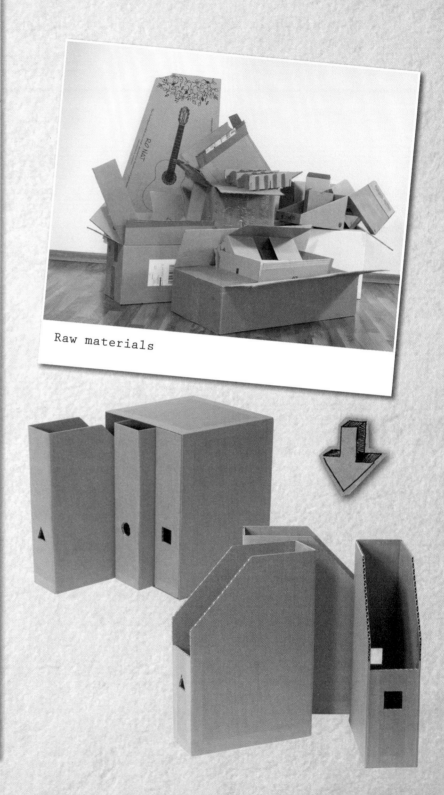

Raw materials

FOUND OBJECTS

Look around:

You can often find interesting objects that can be used for more than just their intended purpose. Found objects can be eye-catching and interesting additions to your pieces.

Those objects with sentimental value that you refuse to part with are well-suited for this purpose. Building them into your projects can give them a life outside of sitting around gathering dust.

It's all a matter of personal taste and style to use an old stereo volume button, the head of an action figure, a well-shaped piece of driftwood, or even a cork as a drawer pull.

Anything is possible—the decision is in your hands! What's good for what use? And for what else?

Hard times ahead for the button-phobic!

LET'S GO SEARCHING!

They're hidden in small junk shops, flea markets, in the back of desk drawers, in the basement or the attic: small treasures perfect for your projects. Nothing lifts the spirits more than finding something exactly right!

A mess? No way! It's a wonderful hodgepodge.

LUMPY, BUTTON-LIKE AND TACTILE:
marbles, stones, plastic pearls,
champagne corks, heads of
plastic figures, small toys from
vending machines, yarn, jewelry
pieces, keyboard parts, toy
building blocks, tree branches
in interesting shapes.

TOOLS AND PROCESSES

Now we'll address the most important tools and processes—the things that are needed for all the projects in this book. You'll get an introduction to all of the techniques, and will come away with the basics of working with cardboard.

Essential: Careful, precise work is your trump card!

The best thing about this book is that if you make a mistake, no expensive material has been wasted. No one should feel demotivated or angry when a cut goes wrong. Minimizing frustrations and staying relaxed leads to more creativity.

Drawing

In order to work precisely with cardboard it's important to first carefully draw out your measurements on the material. This drawing is key for an end result that works. If the measurements and angles are incorrect, no lid will fit and no drawer will slide.

The drawing tools we recommend are a long ruler (50cm, ideally steel, so it can also be used as a cutting guide), a large triangle protractor, a hard (2H) and soft (HB) pencil, an eraser, and a compass.

A helpful drawing tool is a stop. A stop is a long, straight, fixed edge that building material with a straight edge and a triangle protractor can be held against. This way the material is held stable, and the protractor can simply slide left or right along the stop. A stop will help ensure that the protractor is always where it should be, perpendicular to the material's edge.

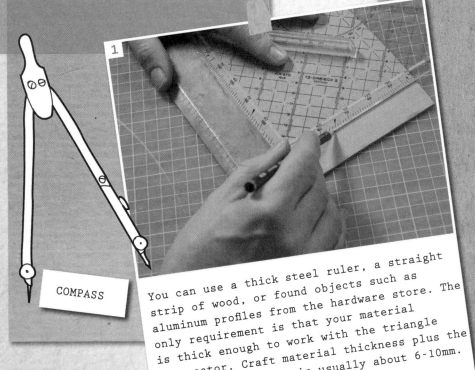

COMPASS

1

You can use a thick steel ruler, a straight strip of wood, or found objects such as aluminum profiles from the hardware store. The only requirement is that your material is thick enough to work with the triangle protractor. Craft material thickness plus the triangle protractor is usually about 6-10mm.

ERASER

2H AND HB PENCIL

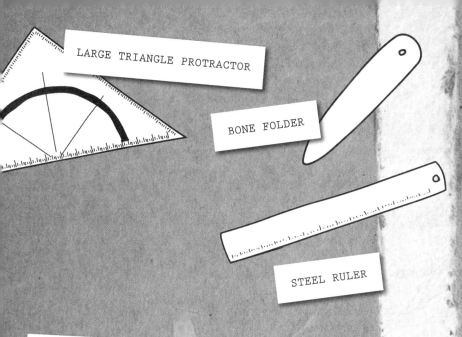

LARGE TRIANGLE PROTRACTOR

BONE FOLDER

STEEL RULER

Folding

To make precise, sharp bent edges with paper and cardboard, first draw a fold line where the fold will be. A fold line can be thought of as a groove in the material and as a mark for folding later on.

We use two types of folds in this book: mountain and valley folds. With a mountain fold, make a groove on the back of the material so that a mountain is formed on the front of the material when it is folded. With a valley fold, the groove is made on the front of the material, and a valley is created.

Building instructions usually show valley folds as dashed lines and mountain folds as dash-dot lines.

Draw your measurements and angles on the material with a sharp pencil. The measurement should always be written in the middle of the line. The points on the drawing don't always need to be connected by lines; it's often enough to score the measurement directly on to the material using a craft knife. The advantage here is that when you need to cut the material, you can place the craft knife in the score mark with the ruler held directly against it. This way you won't need to look for drawn-on marks while cutting.

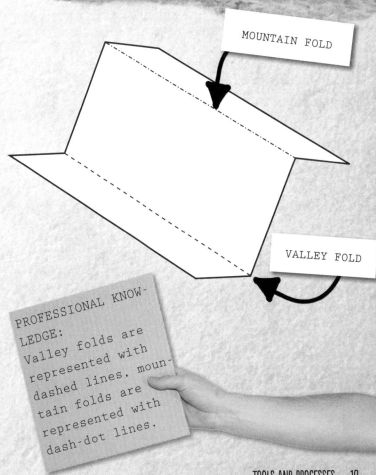

MOUNTAIN FOLD

VALLEY FOLD

PROFESSIONAL KNOW-LEDGE:
Valley folds are represented with dashed lines, mountain folds are represented with dash-dot lines.

Folding thin cardboard:

Beautiful folds can be achieved with the help of a bone folder, guided by a ruler. A bone folder is an old bookbinders' tool made of bone or plastic. Its point is used to make grooves.

The sides of the bone folder can be used to smooth down a fold.

WHAT EXACTLY IS A MITER JOINT?

A miter joint is a beveled 45° edge, such as you often find in everyday life—for example, the edge of a table or a picture frame.

TIP

It's best to make folds before cutting out your pieces. This way you have more room to work and can pull the folds uniformly over the entire piece, rather than trying to fold small, fiddly bits of cardboard.

Folding corrugated cardboard:

1

With corrugated cardboard, folds should be made diagonally to the direction of the corrugation when possible. Otherwise there is a risk of the cardboard not folding accurately.

2

For delicate folding jobs, only use corrugated cardboard up to 2.5mm thick.

3

If you need to fold corrugated cardboard thicker than 2.5mm, it helps to make a deep crease in the material before trying to fold it.

4

The crease will help guide the fold more accurately.

CUTTING

The most important cutting tools for the work in this book are craft knifes with interchangeable blades in two sizes.

The large craft knife (blade width 18mm) is used for cutting material to shape and cutting thick cardboard. The wide blade is well-suited for long, straight cuts.

The small craft knife (blade width 9mm) is better for more delicate jobs.

A wonderful variation is a craft knife with interchangeable 30° blades. The sharper angle of the blade is excellent for very precise work.

FOR BEST RESULTS WHEN CUTTING, BREAK OFF BLADE SEGMENTS BEFORE MAKING IMPORTANT CUTS!

Buying a craft knife:

Pay attention to the blade stopper and metal blade guide when purchasing a craft knife. Don't try to save money on a craft knife—the $5 to $10 is well spent on your safety and precise workmanship. This also applies to blades. Cheap blades go dull very quickly and are often so thin that they go loose and wobble in the holder.

One should use a cutting mat when working with a craft knife. It will protect the work surface as well as the blades of your tools, and ensures a soft cutting guide. Cutting mats come in many different sizes and qualities, but we recommend a self-healing mat at least 18 x 24 inches large.

Working with the craft knife:

After drawing your measurements, place the steel ruler against the markings and cut along the full length, using a small amount of pressure at first. After that, the material can be cut using two or three more cuts with more pressure. Take care that the ruler doesn't slide! When cutting freehand, make several light cuts to ensure the cut is more accurate and avoid messing up your edge.

When cutting, make sure that the blade is at a right angle to the material being cut. You can't construct anything precisely if it has slanted edges. Imprecise cuts stand out and can't be easily concealed, especially with curved pieces.

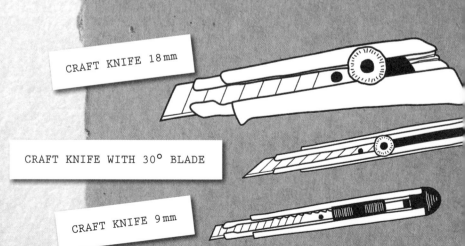

CRAFT KNIFE 18mm

CRAFT KNIFE WITH 30° BLADE

CRAFT KNIFE 9 mm

CIRCLE CUTTER

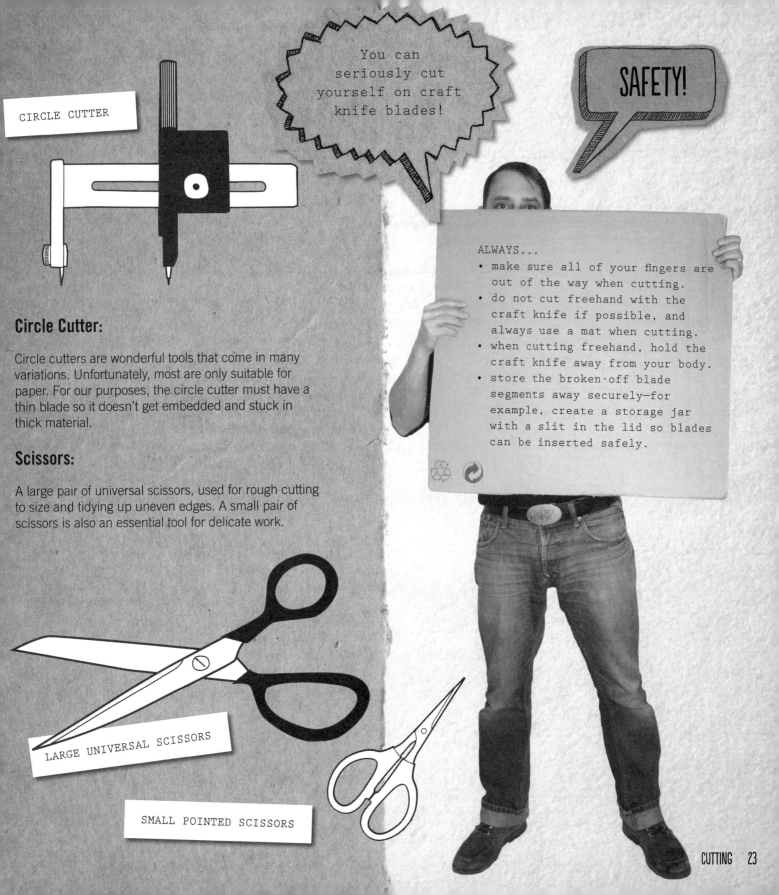

You can seriously cut yourself on craft knife blades!

SAFETY!

Circle Cutter:

Circle cutters are wonderful tools that come in many variations. Unfortunately, most are only suitable for paper. For our purposes, the circle cutter must have a thin blade so it doesn't get embedded and stuck in thick material.

Scissors:

A large pair of universal scissors, used for rough cutting to size and tidying up uneven edges. A small pair of scissors is also an essential tool for delicate work.

ALWAYS...
• make sure all of your fingers are out of the way when cutting.
• do not cut freehand with the craft knife if possible, and always use a mat when cutting.
• when cutting freehand, hold the craft knife away from your body.
• store the broken-off blade segments away securely—for example, create a storage jar with a slit in the lid so blades can be inserted safely.

LARGE UNIVERSAL SCISSORS

SMALL POINTED SCISSORS

GLUING

Glue is the second most important material after cardboard for the projects in this book.

Remember to thin liquid glues before using them on cardboard or paper to be sure you can paint over them later.

Kraft tape:

For the jobs in this book we recommend a commercially available kraft tape. Kraft tape is gummed paper, like postage stamps, which needs to be moistened before use. Kraft tape is available in neutral brown and white rolls of 40mm or 60mm width. In this book we mainly used neutral brown tape rolls 40mm wide. Kraft tape has a few advantages compared to other adhesive tape. It can achieve an exceptionally tight joint between individual pieces while hiding the cut edges; because it is made of paper, it has a homogenous overall effect on cardboard crafts, and objects it is used on can be painted on directly without any problems.

Tips for working with kraft tape can be found from page 26 onward.

Paper patches:

Strips of paper or packaging material can be used as an alternative to kraft tape with the correct application of glue or paste.

Hot glue or masking tape:

For short-term constructions, individual pieces can be joined at concealed points using a hot glue gun. A few strips of re-usable masking tape can also be used to hold pieces together temporarily.

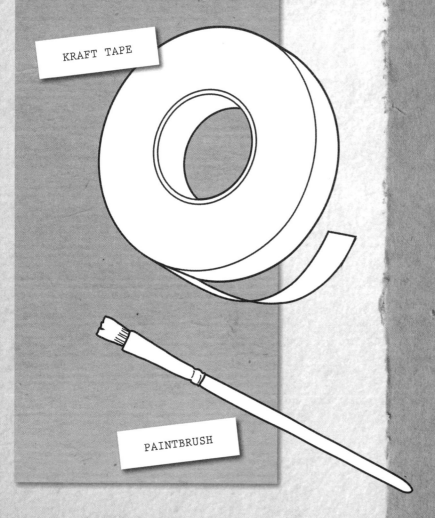

KRAFT TAPE

PAINTBRUSH

Dispersion glue:

Dispersion glue, which can be applied with a wide paintbrush, is well-suited for wide surface areas that will be concealed with paper.

Bookbinding or PVA glue:

Thinned PVA glue works well for gluing delicate, lightweight paper (of low paper weight), tissue paper and cellulose materials (e.g. napkins). Make sure that the dyes in the paper are water-resistant, otherwise there will be quite a mess!

Paint roller:

A paint roller is, of course, usually used to apply and absorb paint. However, it is also a useful tool for applying uniform pressure to layers of paper.

Double-sided kraft tape:

In some of the jobs in this book, it is a good idea to work with double-sided kraft tape. If you don't have it at hand, you can replace it with glue.

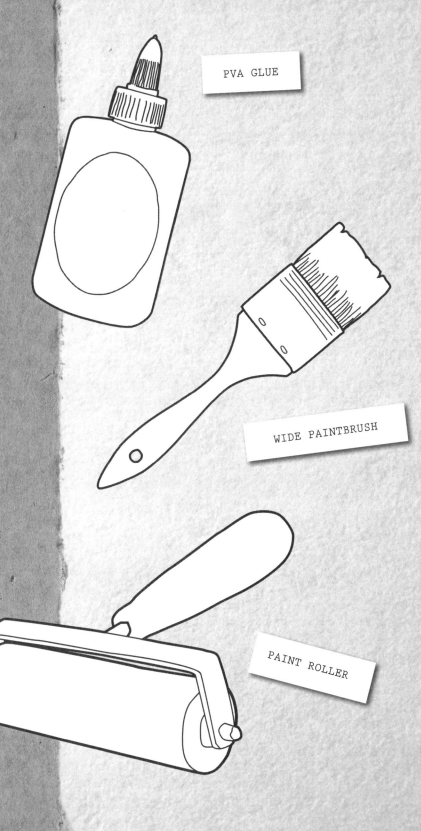

PVA GLUE

WIDE PAINTBRUSH

PAINT ROLLER

USING KRAFT TAPE

The invention of kraft tape has revolutionized our work with paper and cardboard, making the work quicker, sturdier and more precise.

The best thing is, unlike a bottle of glue, kraft tape never dries out!

Required material:

For working with kraft tape, you will need a pair of scissors, a small craft knife, a medium-sized brush and a container of water.

Be aware: kraft tape is very robust on the gummed side and can have a life of its own once unrolled!

First we will show you how to apply kraft tape to an inner corner, and then to an outer corner. Next we will explain how to elegantly conceal the cut edges of corrugated cardboard with adhesive tape. Finally, you will be introduced to the art of gluing over the corner, which is not as difficult as it may seem.

The principle of wet gluing isn't so unusual: it's used on postage stamps and mailing parcels. Gummed paper is also the medium of choice for many street artists. What does this teach us? That gummed kraft tape is indestructible!

Use:

Activate the adhesive tape by moistening it with a paintbrush once or twice at the most. Be careful not to use too much water, but also make sure that the edges of the tape are moist. It's recommended to keep an extra layer between the tape and cutting mat while moistening to keep the gum from getting on the mat.

Handling time:

As soon as the gum is moistened, the paper expands and needs to be used in the next 45 seconds (approximately). If an area doesn't stick after applying the tape, simply moisten it again with the brush and press it back down.

WATER CONTAINER

CUTTING MAT

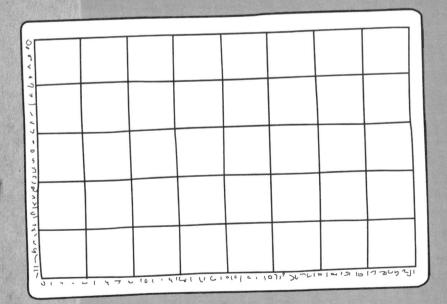

Sticking inner corners:

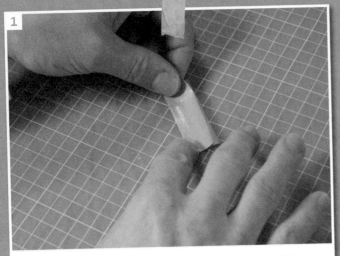

Cut your kraft tape and fold it in half down the middle.

Moisten one half on the gummed side and position it with the brush. Press down, then moisten the other side and push it into the corner using the brush.

Finally, go over the corner with a bone folder to make sure the tape's fold fits snugly into the corner.

TIP

Only wet one half of the tape at a time—moisten the other half once the tape is in place.

Taping outer corners:

KRAFT TAPE

1 First, cut a generous piece of kraft tape. Place the tape over the corners of the cardboard.

2 Place the edge of the adhesive tape parallel to the cardboard and press it on. Cut the tape that extends beyond the corner on the underside.

Thickness of the material

3 Fold over both sides of the cut tape and stick them securely to the bottom.

4 The tape will be cut three times total on the top of the piece: once at the corner, and twice at the same thickness as the cardboard, to the left and the right of the corner.

5

Fold the narrow strip over the edge of the cardboard.

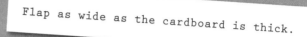

Flap as wide as the cardboard is thick.

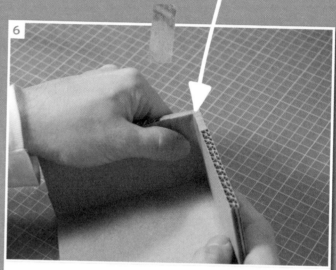

6

The two wide flaps are also folded inwards.

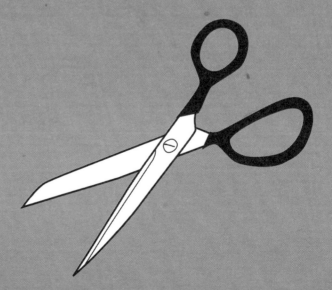

Concealing corners with straight edges:

1 Cut a generous length of tape. Then moisten it down the middle and, while keeping tension on the tape, stick it over the corner onto the cardboard's sides.

2 Using scissors, cut the tape up to the corner joint.

3 Moisten the first of the two flaps and fold it over. Then continue to moisten and fold over the other flaps.

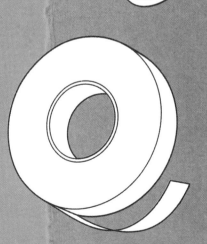

Concealing round edges:

Real boxes have curves!

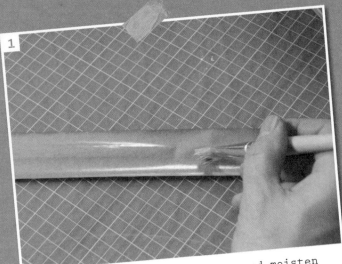

Cut a generous length of tape and moisten it down the middle.

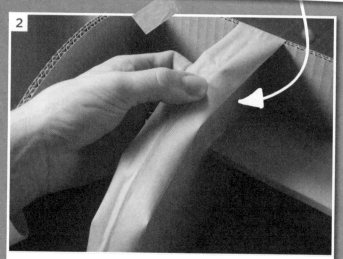

Stick the tape tightly at the center of the round edge.

Firmly stick the upper and lower ends of the tape around the edges of the box, being careful not to lose the tension.

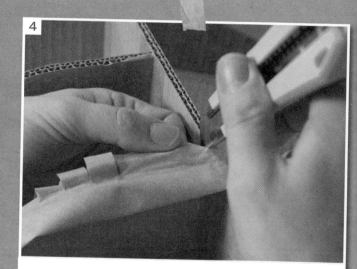

Then, cut the tape into equal-sized sections to make flaps.

5

Now we move on to gluing! Moisten each cut section and stick down every other flap.

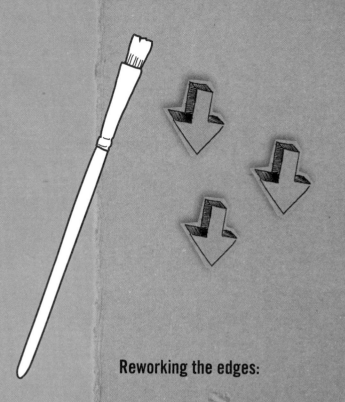

Reworking the edges:

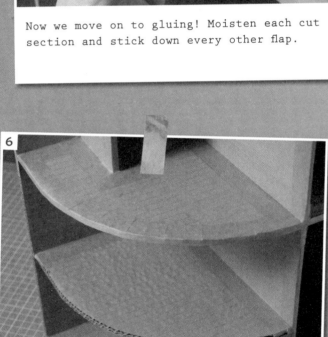

6

Stick the remaining flaps down next. The first curve is now concealed! Don't forget to keep tension in the tape through this process; the light tension will make the taped edges look neater and more attractive.

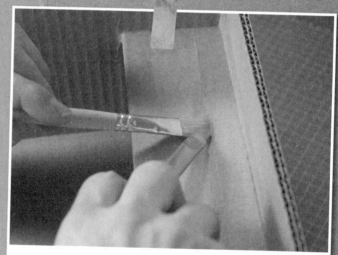

Sometimes the edges of the kraft tape lift up because they have not been sufficiently moistened. If this happens, raise them gently with the blade of a craft knife, moisten them with a paintbrush and press them into place again.

CHAPTER 2

FINISHES

COVERING WITH PAPER

In our experience, we found that uncoated, ordinary, natural paper together with a relatively viscous elastic dispersion glue worked best for covering entire boxes. Coated paper tends to become wavy after the glue has dried when it is used to cover large surface areas. On the other hand, coated paper can be glued to small areas and narrow strips without any problems.

COATED VS. UNCOATED PAPER — HOW CAN I TELL THE DIFFERENCE?

Materials & Tools

- ☐ Object to be covered
- ☐ Uncoated or natural paper
- ☐ Elastic dispersion glue

- ☐ Ruler
- ☐ Triangle protractor
- ☐ Pencil
- ☐ Craft knife
- ☐ Wide brush

Uncoated paper is also called natural paper. It has a coarse surface that is very absorbent. In contrast, coated paper, such as craft paper or photo paper, has a finished surface for achieving better quality photographic prints. The "coat" is a special application that gives the paper a smooth, non-absorbent finish.

It's best to apply the glue evenly on a flat surface. Wait until the paper is soaked through before sticking it to the object.

COVERING AN ENTIRE BOX:

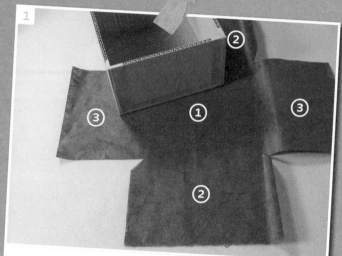

① ② ③

Draw the measurements of the box, including the sticking flaps as per the drawing, onto the paper and cut it out.

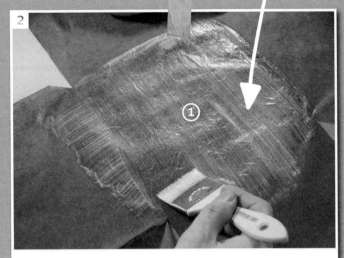

BOTTOM

①

Brush the bottom side of the paper with glue and allow it to soak through.

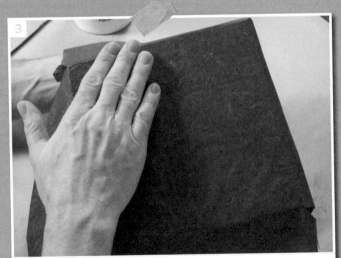

Stick the bottom side to the box.

Attach the side parts in order.

The corners are treated as explained on p. 28.

Let the finished work dry well.

COVERING PARTS OF A BOX:

GLUING THIN AND CELLULOSE PAPER:

Smaller pieces of coated paper can be attached with dispersion glue by thoroughly soaking them with glue. Strips of a road map are well-suited for this, for example.

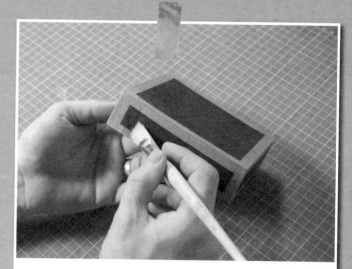

Pieces of coated paper can be glued well with thin PVA glue or tissue paste. It's best to first coat the area you want to stick things to with glue. Then position the paper where you want it and brush over it with more glue. With some glues this will also make the surface water resistant.

COVERING WITH FABRIC

Fabric can be used as a covering in almost exactly the same way as paper. There is only one difference: here, the box is brushed with glue. If it is done the other way around the fabric could color the glue, which could be quite unattractive.

Any material that can be folded is suitable for this. Thicker, more stubborn material should be folded and ironed at the folds before attempting to glue it.

MATERIALS & TOOLS

- ☐ Object to be covered
- ☐ Foldable or folded and ironed fabric
- ☐ Elastic dispersion glue
- ☐ Clothespins

- ☐ Ruler
- ☐ Triangle Protractor
- ☐ Pencil
- ☐ Craft knife and scissors
- ☐ Wide brush

Covering a box with fabric:

Draw the box measurements in accordance with the drawing on p. 41 and cut out the fabric.

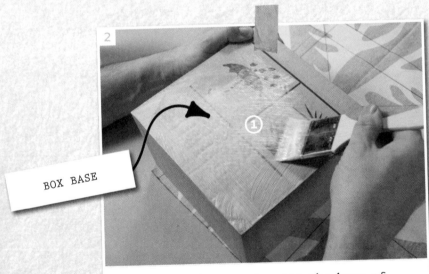

BOX BASE

Brush the glue evenly onto the base of the box.

Keep going on page 42

TIP

When covering a box with fabric, apply the glue to the cardboard, not the fabric.

COVERING A BOX WITH FABRIC:

Place the base of the box on the fabric and carefully press the two together.

BOTTOM

Brush the sides of the box with glue and stick the wide flaps on each side to their corresponding sides ②.

Glue the corners as explained on pages 28–29.

SIDES ③

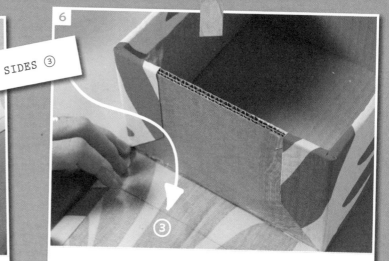

Brush the flaps on the side ③ with glue and fold them over.

7

Brush the box sides ③ with glue, stick the side parts on and hold the glued fabric on the sides in place with small clothespins while they dry.

8

Once the outside is covered it's up to you whether or not to dress up the inside.

PRINTING WITH STYROFOAM

Printing with styrofoam is simple, and produces eye-catching results.

This technique is suitable for small prints as well as printing larger surfaces. Styrofoam containers can often be found in the food sections of supermarkets—for example, as fruit and meat trays, or as take-away boxes. The necessity of a thorough cleaning before reusing them goes without saying.

MATERIALS & TOOLS

- ☐ Object to be printed
- ☐ Styrofoam container
- ☐ Color (for example, acrylic paint or linocut ink)

- ☐ Ruler
- ☐ Blunt pencil and 2B pencil
- ☐ Craft knife
- ☐ Wide brush or paint roller

These beautiful patterns attract all kinds of animals...

...and even exotic species!

Dip the paint roller in the color.

The raised parts will be what are colored.

Parts of the printing surface are depressed, so they don't get any color in them. The areas that are raised take on the color, and will be the colored parts in the print. Thus we are working with a relief printing process.

Preparing the relief:

Choose a suitable piece of styrofoam. You can only use the flat parts of the container for printing.

Cut the piece you want to use in a way that lets you make the most of the surface.

Next, cut the surface to fit the area that will be printed.

Making the relief:

4

Use a blunt pencil to press a motif into the material. You can either work freehand or use a 2B pencil to carefully draw out the motif first.

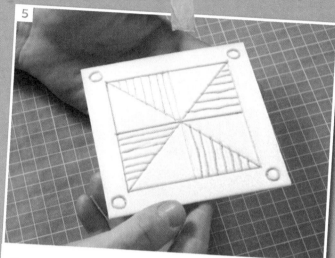

5

In the finished motif, the lines that are depressed will be the ones without color in the final print. The raised areas will stamp the color on the space that is to be printed.

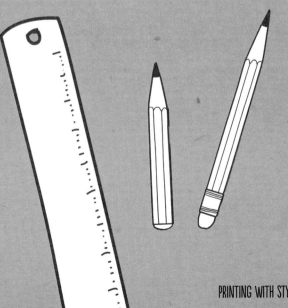

Coloring and stamping:

Evenly apply the color to the printing plate with a paint roller or brush.

The color will spread on to the raised parts of the printing plate, leaving the depressions clean.

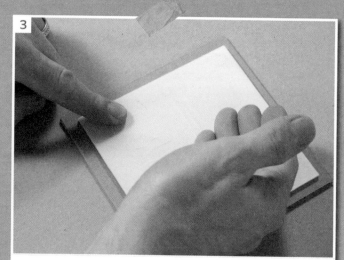

Press the printing plate on to the area to be printed. Make sure to apply even pressure over the plate.

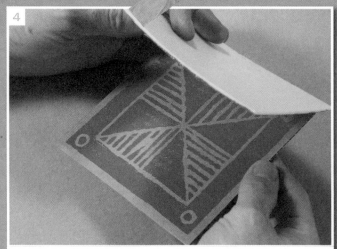

Lift the printing plate off carefully.

First print the top...

...of the box...

...beautiful results!

Ready-made boxes and lids can also be printed. Just make sure that the printing plate works properly first.

...let it dry...

...print the sides...

STAMPING

Small stamps can be made from a variety of materials, and give you the freedom to create the texture you want. Cork, plastic padding from packaging, styrofoam (as just shown), rubber, and of course, potatoes!

MATERIALS & TOOLS

- ☐ Unused stamp (for example, cork or rubber padding plate)
- ☐ Color (for example, acrylic paint or linocut ink)

- ☐ Craft knife
- ☐ Brush or paint roller

Constructing small cork stamps:

Trim the end of your stamp flat.

Draw your motif, then sculpt out the end of your stamp. Don't use pens or markers with washable or erasable ink to draw the motif.

Coloring and stamping:

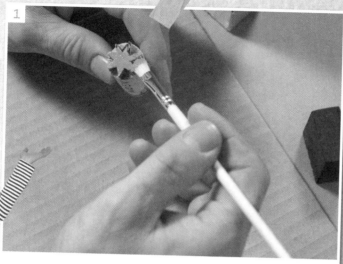

1

Carefully and thoroughly cover the printing end of the stamp with a brush.

TIP

When covering the stamp with a color, make sure it doesn't seep into gaps in the stamp.

2

Now stamp it!

Making a patterned stamp from a rubber pad:

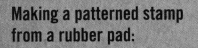

1 Cut a pattern freehand into the rubber pad.

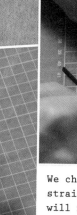

2 We chose a pattern of intersecting straight lines. Small, neat squares will make up the print.

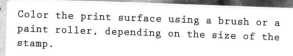

3 Color the print surface using a brush or a paint roller, depending on the size of the stamp.

4 Press the stamp onto the area to be printed.

5 Several small prints can make up a large pattern.

VARNISHING AND PAINTING

In general, corrugated cardboard is difficult to paint without thinning the colors. Before you proceed with painting your finished product, you should always test your paint on a spare piece of the same material. You may discover new and unknown effects.

Small areas can be painted with a brush. A good contrast to the base tone can be achieved with a Chinese White acrylic color.

Corrugated cardboard is very sensitive to water, and small bumps will appear on the surface if water-based products like acrylic paint and dispersion ink are used on large areas. These textures are so regular that they could almost be used as a pattern in their own right.

Corrugated cardboard can be painted easily with spray paint! Several thin layers of paint will produce a rich, vibrant color.

CHAPTER 3

BOXES

SQUARE BOX

Everyone needs boxes. You can use them to hide clutter, sort bits and pieces, store your CD and DVD collections or replace drawers in a wardrobe. Old love letters belong in a box, as do receipts for next year's taxes. Boxes bring order to a messy person's life; an order fanatic's heart races when they see them. You simply can't have enough boxes!

Boxes aren't only practical—they can also be beautiful. They're fantastic for gifts that have no straight edges and can't be easily wrapped. They can be reused, and don't wander off after being handed over to the recycling bin.

Try making your own boxes when you need to store a lot of items that are all the same size. Or if you want to fill that odd little gap in the hall closet with a perfectly-sized box, or if your collection of teabags needs a new home, or, or, or...Surely we all have thousands of things that could be stored away in a better way!

ATTENTION

When using corrugated cardboard for boxes, the corrugations in the side walls must run vertically (from top to bottom): otherwise you won't be able to make accurate edges.

Many of the projects in this book are variations on the square box shown here. Depending on the thickness of the material, there are three different possibilities when making this type of box. So first, you must measure the thickness of your cardboard.

Construction variations according to thickness of material:

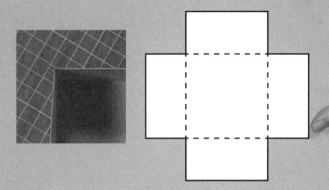

1 For paper or greyboard up to 0.5mm thick, cut, fold and attach the pieces according to the measurements (LxWxH).

x = THICKNESS OF MATERIAL

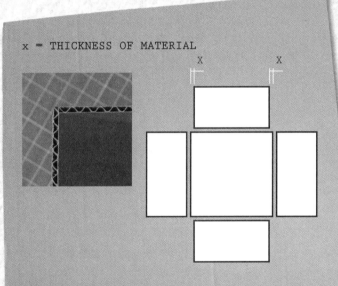

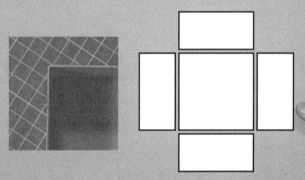

2 If you use material between 0.5 and 1mm thick, cut the pieces to measure and assemble them edge-to-edge using kraft tape.

3 When using material thicker than 1mm, cut the sides in such a way that the longer sides can extend past the shorter sides (see drawing: measure X is the thickness of the material) and stick together with kraft tape. By following this method you can work accurately even with thick cardboard.

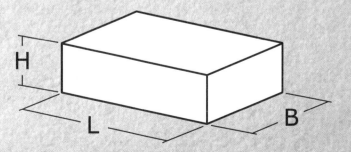

SQUARE-BASED

Over the next few pages we'll show you how to make a small square box, its lid, and several variations. There are several different ways to construct this box, depending on its intended use and your personal preferences. It's up to you to decide on the dimensions; the important thing is that the ratio of the sides is correct.

The projects in this chapter almost exclusively use 2.5mm corrugated cardboard, so be sure to use variation 3 from the styles shown on page 56. In the top view on the right you can see that the short side pieces are cut to a smaller width to allow for the thickness of the cardboard.

MATERIAL & Tools

For all projects you always need:

- ☐ Sufficiently large cardboard
- ☐ Kraft tape
- ☐ Craft knife and cutting mat
- ☐ Scissors
- ☐ Pencils
- ☐ Ruler
- ☐ Stop
- ☐ Triangle Protractor
- ☐ Brush and water container

CUTTING THE CARDBOARD:

Individual parts for a box of 130 x 130 x 65mm (LxWxH) made from 2.5mm thick corrugated cardboard

- ☐ 1 x base - 130 x 130mm
- ☐ 2 x long side parts 130 x 62.5mm
- ☐ 2 x short side parts less double the thickness of the material, so 125 x 62.5mm

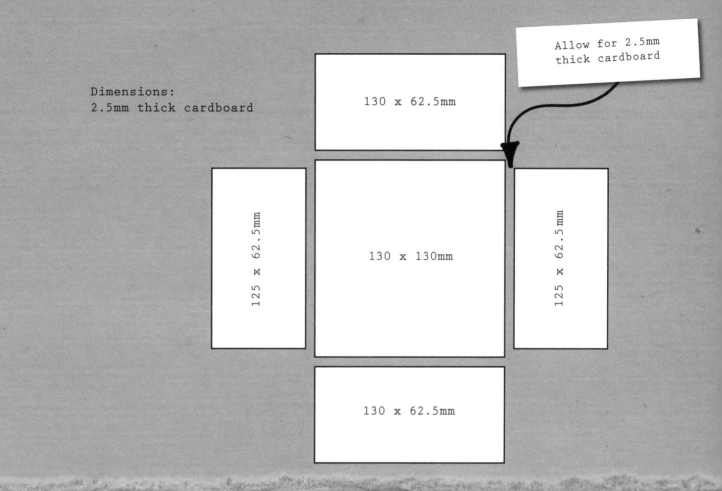

Dimensions:
2.5mm thick cardboard

130 x 62.5mm

Allow for 2.5mm thick cardboard

125 x 62.5mm

130 x 130mm

125 x 62.5 mm

130 x 62.5mm

MAKING YOUR OWN BOX:

You want to build a box that follows your own measurements?

No problem! If you want to make a box that measures 300 x 100 x 50mm (LxWxH), for example, you'll need the following parts:

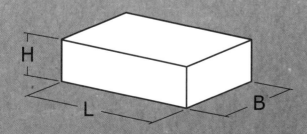

Base: 300 x 100mm (L x B)

Front: 300 x 50mm (L x H)

Side parts: 100 x 50mm (H x B)

Building the square box:

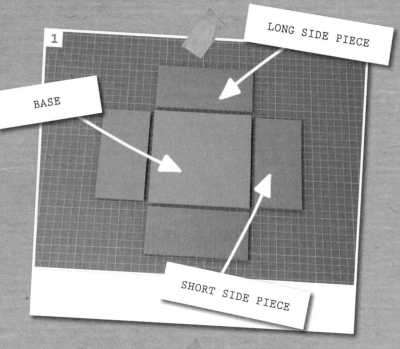

1

BASE

LONG SIDE PIECE

SHORT SIDE PIECE

2

BASE

Stick kraft tape all the away around the base.

3

LONG SIDE PART

Now place the long side pieces edge-to-edge against the base. It's often helpful to lean the base upright against an object to help steady it. This can be anything that can sit at a 90° to the base and is sturdy enough to balance the cardboard that leans against it. Another box works well for this, or, as in our photo, a square paperweight.

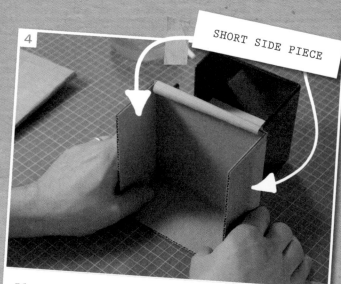

4

SHORT SIDE PIECE

Place the short side pieces between the long ones.

5

Tape all of the side pieces together. This is the time to conceal the top edges of the sides, if you'd like to do that.

6

Cut the top end of the adhesive tape...

7

...and fold it inwards.

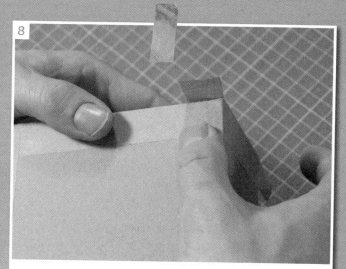

8

Cut the tape at the bottom corners and fold it over...and you're done!

BOX WITH COMPARTMENTS

Dividers allow you to make a box that fits your individual needs. You can securely store small or delicate pieces in the compartments, such as jewelry, writing utensils, or camera equipment.

Cut slits into pieces of thin cardboard and slot them together to make dividers. Slits that are a little thinner than the thickness of the cardboard will give you the most stability when the dividers are put together. Prepare them outside of the box and insert the dividers as a whole into the box when it is finished.

Make slits partway into pieces of thin cardboard to make dividers.

Inserting and concealing thin dividers:

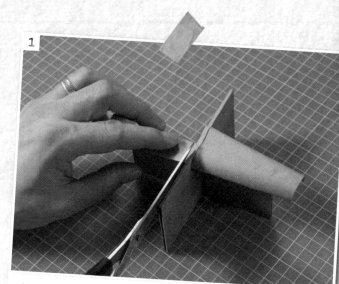

After cutting, place a piece of kraft tape over the top of divider and cut the tape at the intersection.

Moisten the adhesive tape and flatten it downward over the top of the divider.

3

Insert the finished dividers into the box.

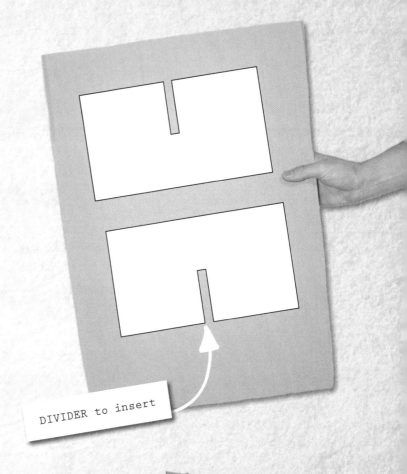

DIVIDER to insert

4

Fix the dividers to the inside of the box with kraft tape. You can reach into the corners using a small brush or bone folder.

5

Fold the protruding ends of the kraft tape used to attach the dividers out over the edge of the box and flatten them down.

BOX WITH
COMPARTMENTS

Dividers made from thicker cardboard are assembled out of individual pieces. Here, the long divider is positioned in the box first, followed by the smaller ones. Everything is then covered with kraft tape. The finished result looks like it was created like that, rather than being a patchwork of cardboard.

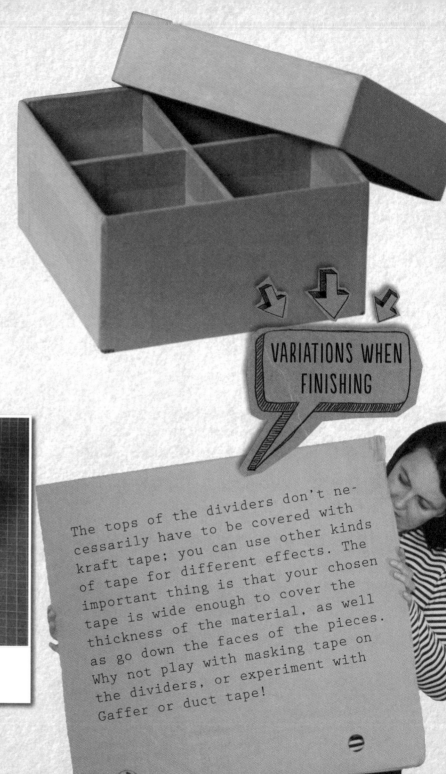

VARIATIONS WHEN FINISHING

The tops of the dividers don't necessarily have to be covered with kraft tape; you can use other kinds of tape for different effects. The important thing is that your chosen tape is wide enough to cover the thickness of the material, as well as go down the faces of the pieces. Why not play with masking tape on the dividers, or experiment with Gaffer or duct tape!

When you use thicker corrugated cardboard attach the dividers inside the box.

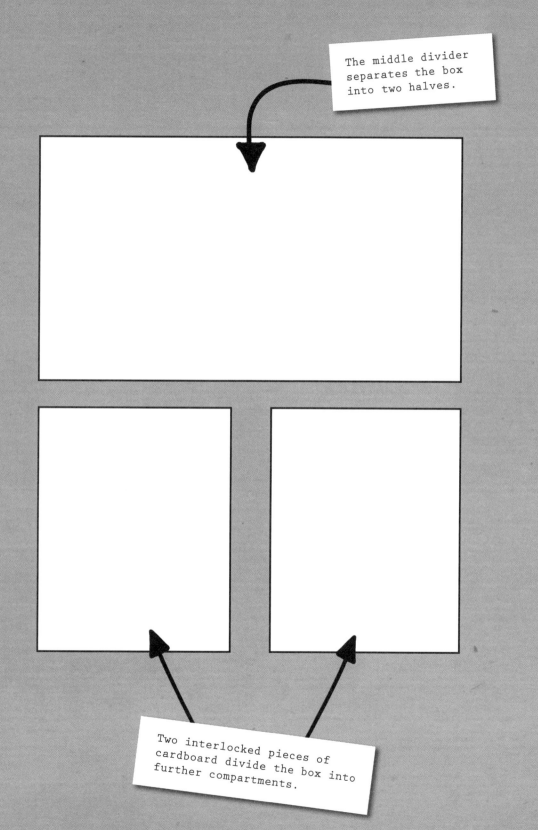

The middle divider separates the box into two halves.

Two interlocked pieces of cardboard divide the box into further compartments.

Inserting and concealing thick dividers:

1 Crease the kraft tape before you start. This way it's ready to be used immediately.

2 Attach the middle divider on the inside for the first division.

3 When the middle divider is firmly in place inside the box, you can insert further segments.

4 Cover the segments with kraft tape and stick it down. The ends of the tape are stuck to the center divider and the outside of the box.

5 Cut the tape at the insides of corners and attach it inwards. Now the box's small segments are concealed.

6 Now for the middle divider. Again, you need to place the full length of tape over the divider, then fold and stick it over the outside of the box.

7 Do the same for the adjacent segments; cut the tape and flatten it inward.

8 Beautifully concealed dividers with four practical compartments!

GIFT BOX

Do you have nosy neighbors? Or a surprise that needs to be hidden away until the right moment? Secret treasures? Cleary, you need a lid!

This lid is made exactly the same way as the basic box, and from the same materials as the box.

In order to get a lid that fits—one that doesn't get stuck, or is too loose—you need to make it a little bigger than the outer measurements of the box, but not by much. For small boxes, with an edge length of 150-200mm, add approximately 2mm to the measurements; bigger boxes will need an addition of approximately 4-5mm.

Making the gift box:

1 Measure the outside of the finished box.

2 Add the extra measurement to the length and width of your box and you'll have the internal measurements of the lid.

EXAMPLE:

Box 130 x 130mm

Addition = 2mm

Lid's internal measurement: 132 x 132mm

3 Draw and cut the base and sides.

EXAMPLE:

Cardboard thickness: 2.5mm
Lid's internal measurements: 132 x 132mm

Lid = 137 x 137mm (internal measurements + 2 x the thickness of the material)

Short sides: Length = 132mm

Long sides: Length = 137mm

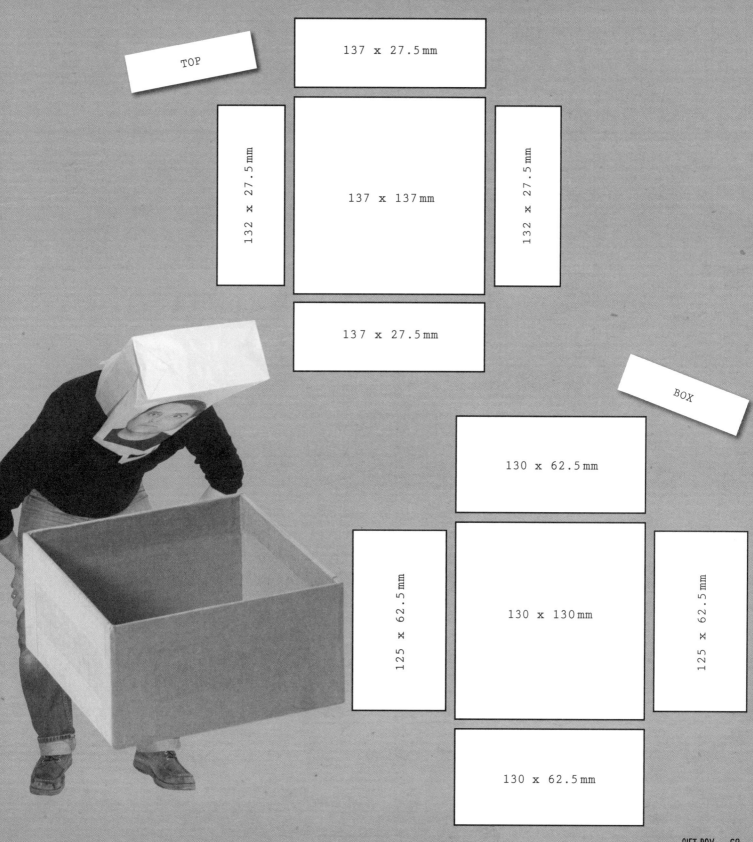

TOP

137 x 27.5mm

132 x 27.5mm

137 x 137mm

132 x 27.5mm

137 x 27.5mm

BOX

130 x 62.5mm

125 x 62.5mm

130 x 130mm

125 x 62.5mm

130 x 62.5mm

WITH FLUSH LID

The flush lid of the gift box is an interior extension of the box that can't be seen from the outside. The box and its lid are flush; the lip between the box and lid is inserted invisibly inside the box in the form of a built frame.

WIDE SIDE PIECE + LID

NARROW SIDE PIECE

To avoid mistakes, it's recommended to draw and cut all the parts needed for the box and lid in one go.

The lid has the same dimensions as the box, other than its height.

The measurements of the interior frame are taken from the inside of the finished box.

The frame can be made of the same material as the lid or of thinner greyboard. Attach it inside with PVA glue or double-sided adhesive tape.

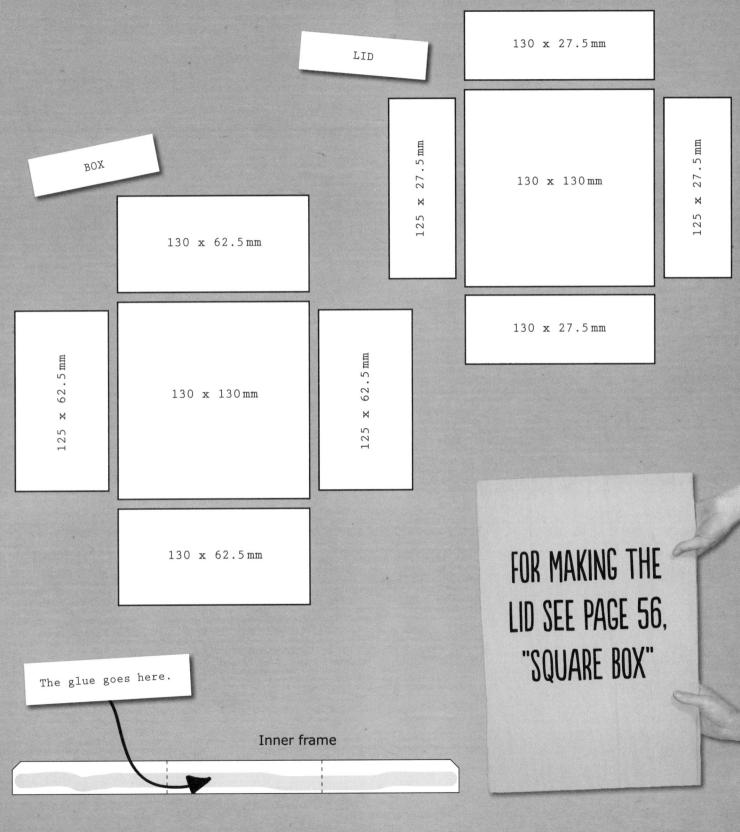

LID

130 x 27.5mm

125 x 27.5 mm

130 x 130mm

125 x 27.5 mm

130 x 27.5mm

BOX

130 x 62.5mm

125 x 62.5 mm

130 x 130mm

125 x 62.5 mm

130 x 62.5mm

FOR MAKING THE LID SEE PAGE 56, "SQUARE BOX"

The glue goes here.

Inner frame

WITH HINGE

The hinged lid is made similarly to the gift box, but there are two differences between them. The hinged lid has a smaller inner frame that serves only as a guide for the lid, and there are hinges on the long side of the box.

The inner frame needs only to be high enough to guide the lid. If it is too high, the lid will get stuck and won't close. You don't need the inner frame on the hinged side.

CUTTING, SEE P. 71

Making the hinged variation:

The hinge for the lid can be easily made by placing two strips of kraft tape on precise spots between the lid and the box. The first piece of tape goes on the back.

Place the second strip of kraft tape on the inside of the joint between the opened lid and the back of the box.

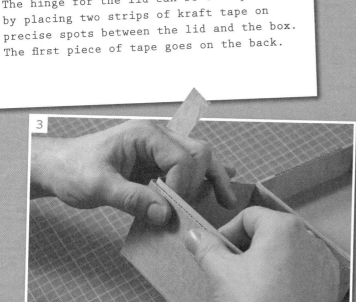

The kraft tape is strong enough to withstand a lot of opening and closing. For even better durability, and a classy look, you can also use a strip of self-adhesive linen on the outside of the box. Many craft stores sell fabric tape in a variety of different colors.

The inner frame serves as a stop for the lid. It guides it, so to speak, into place.

TREASURE CHEST

Treasure chests aren't just for pirates. You can store all sorts of special items in them, big or small.

Corrugated cardboard isn't really suited for making the curved surface of the lid of this box. It creases badly along the corrugations and won't form a curved bow. It's better to use a 0.5mm thick greyboard.

ATTENTION

Greyboard is more pliable and bends easier when folded perpendicular to the direction of the grain!

WHAT ARE YOU HIDING IN YOUR TREASURE CHEST?

HALF THE CIRCLE CIRCUMFERENCE = Pi (3.141…) x diameter
2

HALF THE WIDTH OF THE BOX MINUS THICKNESS OF THE MATERIAL OF THE CURVED AREA

Making the treasure chest lid:

1

Before assembling the lid, you need to prepare the piece that will bend over the curved sides in order to prevent it from warping from the tension. The bone folder will help you here. Cut the side pieces (that have already been cut to the width of the box) down double the thickness of the material you're using for the curved area. (For instance, if the curved material is 0.5mm, remove 1mm from each side piece.)

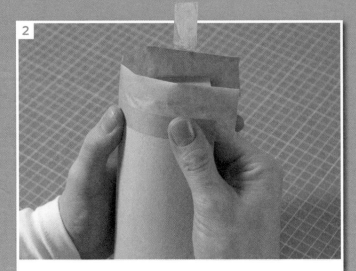

2

Attach kraft tape to the edge of the curved area.

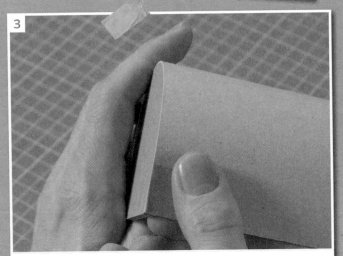

3

Make sure that the edges of the curved area are flush with the side pieces.

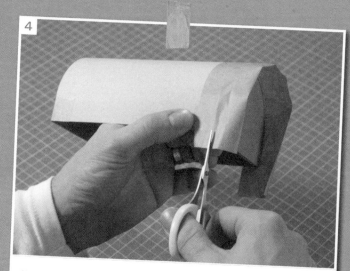

4

Now we will cut the kraft tape prior to gluing it. First cut down the center of the ends that protrude over the edge of the lid.

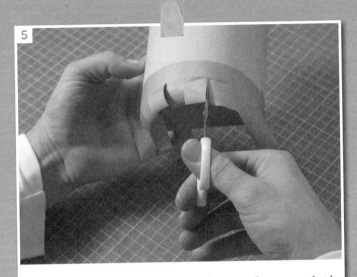

Next, cut flaps at regular intervals around the curve of the lid.

Note: When sticking the flaps, first attach every other flap, then follow up with the rest.

The flaps of kraft tape will overlap somewhat along the curve of the lid. This will increase the lid's stability.

STACKABLE BOXES

A stackable box can be made from as many basic boxes as you like. The lid will go on the very top box. Obviously the wider and flatter the boxes, the more of them you can stack.

Stacking follows an insertion principle that allows you to go on almost indefinitely. You can always put one more box on top!

As for the gift box on page 70, it makes sense to cut all the side pieces in one step for this project. This will help you avoid inaccuracies when making the boxes, and will make the silhouette of the stacked box smoother.

Stack individual boxes with simple cardboard sides 6mm thick. The sides should fit snugly to the protruding base of the box above as a guide.

Joining the stackable boxes:

The panels for the pieces that will join the boxes are cut from thick cardboard. The panels should be 1-2mm smaller than the inner measurements of the boxes. Glue the panel (or use double-sided adhesive tape) to the center of the box's base. No panel goes on the bottom of the bottom box.

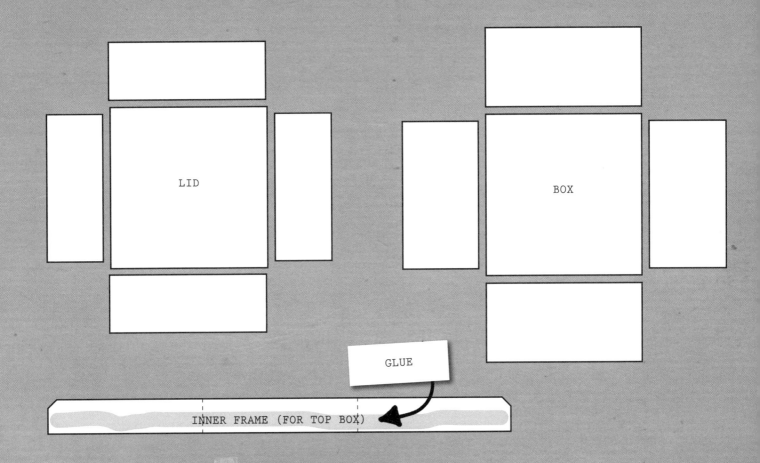

LID

BOX

GLUE

INNER FRAME (FOR TOP BOX)

JOINING
PANEL

2

It looks especially good when you conceal the edges of the panels with kraft tape. This also has an advantage in that it prevents wear and tear of the edges. If you decide to conceal the edges, make sure to cut the joining panels half a millimeter smaller.

HOUSE OF BOOKS

The "House of Books" can be used as a "parking space" for books, a bookmark, or just for storing whatever's on your bedside table.

The construction is simple: first, make a base with two 90° gables on opposite ends. You can add inner compartments if you like.

It's best to make the house 15 x 18cm for hardcover books and paperbacks; the size can be easily adjusted to accommodate larger books.

The shape of the book open atop this project reminded us strongly of the roof on a house. This is an invitation to get creative! With a little work...

90°-GABLE

...it can also have a door for visitors!

...a round hole and a perch at the front turn your "House of Books" into a bird house!

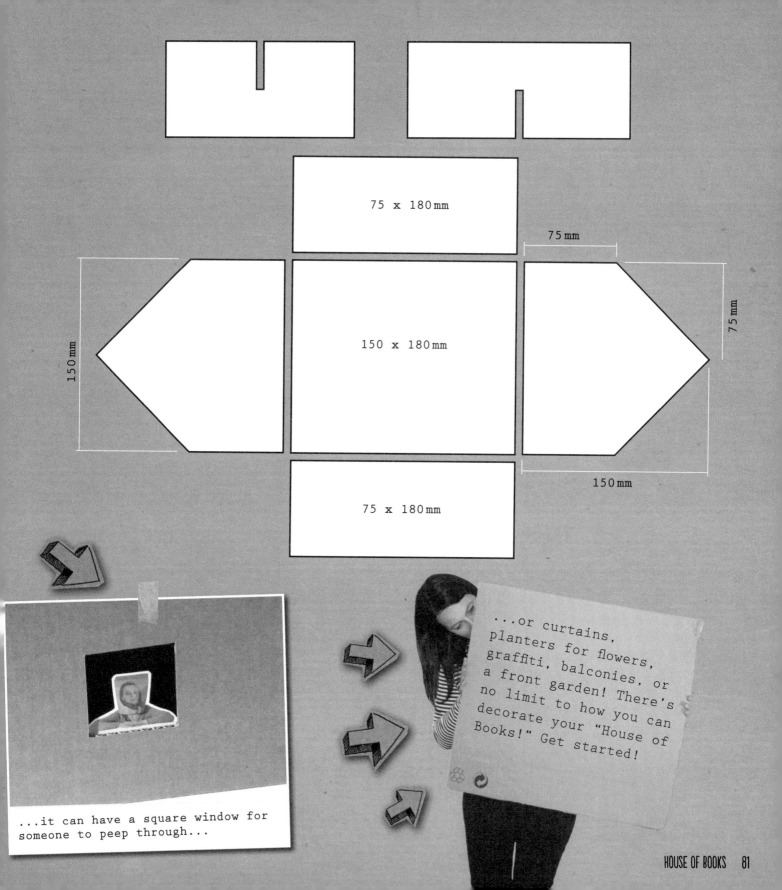

75 x 180mm

75 mm

150 mm

150 x 180mm

75 mm

75 x 180mm

150mm

...it can have a square window for someone to peep through...

...or curtains, planters for flowers, or graffiti, balconies, or a front garden! There's no limit to how you can decorate your "House of Books!" Get started!

ROUND BOX

The second basic shape for a box is round. Round boxes are a bit less practical than square ones, but they're much more decorative. They're perfect for precious items that deserve more elaborate packaging.

Because of their nature, round boxes are constructed differently than square ones. Before you start, you need to calculate the circumference of your box with this formula:

Circumference = Pi (3.141…) x diameter

The circumference of a box with a diameter of 130mm is calculated like this:

3.141 x 130 (circumference) = 408.33. Use the rounded up result 409.

The best material to use for the side walls of round boxes is greyboard. Corrugated cardboard will crease, as we saw with the treasure chest, and won't produce a smooth, curved shape.

Making the round box:

1 Cut the material:

Individual parts for a box 130 x 65mm (D x H):

1 base with diameter of 130mm (any material)
1 side wall 409mm (circumference) x 65mm (0.5mm greyboard)

2 Prepare the side wall (see "Treasure Chest," p. 74)

SIDE WALL 409 x 65mm

BASE
Ø 130mm

Memorizing the digits of Pi is a great way to impress and annoy your friends and family. A good way to start is with a short Pi poem—a "piem"—in which the number of letters in the words corresponds to the digits in Pi. For instance: "Pie, I wish I could recollect Pi!" = 3.141592

Making the round box:

1 Tape the side piece together so that it forms a tube.

2 Tape all the way around the side of the tube, leaving plenty of tape over the edge to attach to the base.

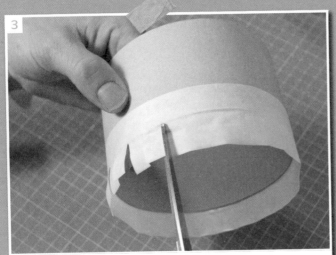

3 Cut the protruding tape all the way around at regular intervals.

4 Fold the tape flaps down toward the outside of the tube.

5

Carefully place the tube on the base. Make sure the bottom of the tube and the edge of the base are flush.

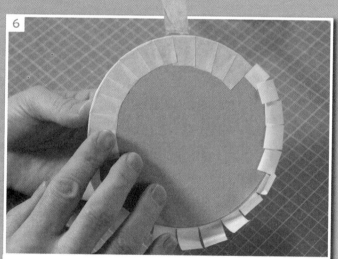

6

Flip it over and press the tape flaps down on the base, keeping some tension in the flaps.

TIP

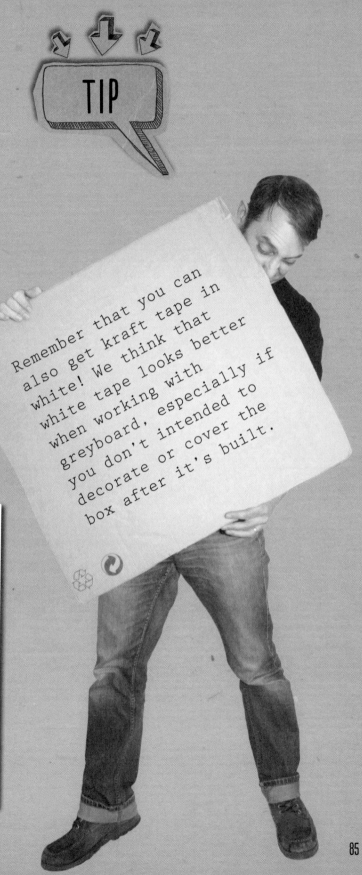

Remember that you can also get kraft tape in white! We think that white tape looks better when working with greyboard, especially if you don't intended to decorate or cover the box after it's built.

WITH FLUSH LID

The lid of this round box is made using the same diameter as the box.

The length of the inner lip should be adjusted and glued to the inside of the box.

LET'S GET ROUND!

AN INNER FRAME AS ON PAGE 70

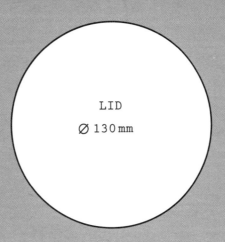

LID

∅ 130 mm

SIDE OF LID 409 x 30 mm

INNER LIP 402 x 15 mm

SIDE OF BOX 409 x 65 mm

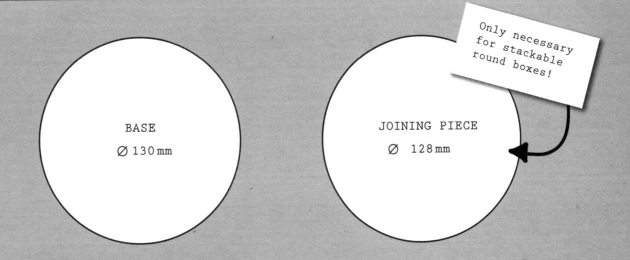

BASE

∅ 130 mm

JOINING PIECE

∅ 128 mm

Only necessary
for stackable
round boxes!

ROUND GIFT BOX

Make the box first, then measure it for the diamater of the lid. This way you avoid making the lid the wrong size.

Add 2mm to the diameter of the box to get the correct size for a lid that fits over the box.

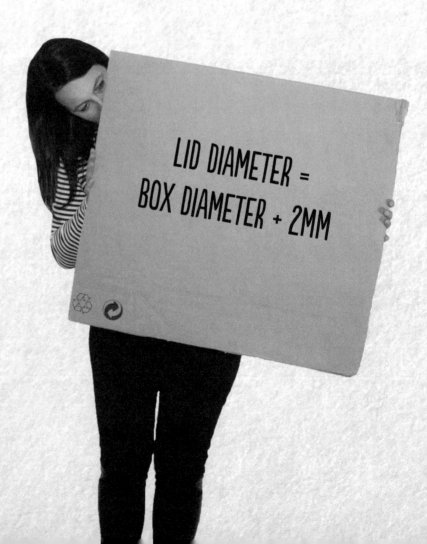

LID DIAMETER = BOX DIAMETER + 2MM

STACKABLE BOX

The stackable round box works just like the square one. Just like the square box, you can stack as many round boxes as you like—the flatter and wider the boxes, the more you can stack. Stack them all the way to the ceiling if you want!

As always, when you need identical pieces, it's recommended to cut them all out in one go. That way you can be sure they all have the same measurements and there are no inaccuracies.

To join the stackable boxes, cut out round panels with a diameter slightly smaller than the inner diameter of the boxes. You can conceal the edges of the panel with kraft tape if you like, then glue the pieces to the bottom of the boxes that will be stacked.

CUTTING, SEE
PAGE 87

CHAPTER 4

DESKTOP

NESTING PEN HOLDER

This "nesting" piece is easy to make. It consists of just three nested cardboard containers and a large base.

MATERIALS & TOOLS

- ☐ Corrugated cardboard (2.5mm)
- ☐ Kraft tape

- ☐ Craft knife
- ☐ Ruler
- ☐ Triangle Protractor
- ☐ Pencil

I CAN STORE YOUR PENS!

Construction:

This piece is built from the inside out.

1 Cut and glue the inner and middle parts first. The larger containers will hold the smaller ones. If you like, you can cover the cut edges with kraft tape.

2 Cut and glue the outer part, including the base. When you're finished, conceal the edges with tape.

3 Insert the middle section into the outer section and fix it in place using kraft tape (see "Basics, Kraft Tape").

4 Insert the inner section into the middle section and attach it to the base by taping it down on the inside.

45 mm 45 mm   40 mm 40 mm

120 mm

MIDDLE SECTION

INNER
SECTION

OUTER SECTION

INNER SECTION
Two parts at 45 x 120mm
Two parts at 40 x 120mm

75 mm   75 mm

70 mm   65 mm

MIDDLE SECTION
Two parts at 70 x 75mm
Two parts at 65 x 75mm

42.5 mm   42.5 mm

105 mm   100 mm

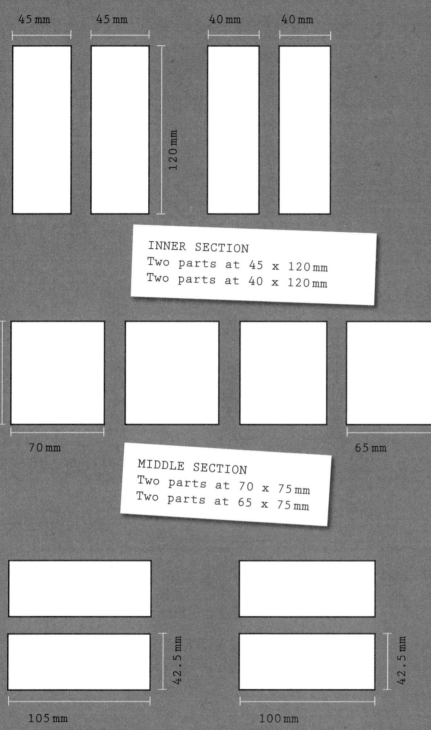

BASE

105 x 105mm

OUTER SECTIONS
Two parts at 105 x 42.5mm
Two parts at 100 x 42.5mm

CUTOUT PEN HOLDER

The "cut out" construction method helps you get the most out of a pen holder. The "sandwich" method of construction makes it possible to make any shallow space you could think of, with all kinds of channels and grooves for all the things you could ever want to neatly store away.

Plan gaps in the sides for standard-sized bits and pieces, like Post-It® notes, pens, erasers, paper clips... anything!

MATERIAL & TOOLS

- ☐ Corrugated cardboard (6 mm)
- ☐ Greyboard (0.5–1mm)
- ☐ PVA glue, Dispersion glue

- ☐ Craft knife
- ☐ Ruler
- ☐ Triangle Protractor
- ☐ Pencil

POST-IT® POCKET

Construction:

1 Plan your "cut out" desk organizer by first determining the outer dimensions, as well as the size and position of the gaps for your Post-It® notes, pens, erasers, and other supplies.

2 Determine how many layers of the 6mm cardboard you'll need in order to achieve the height you want and cut the outer measurements of the base.

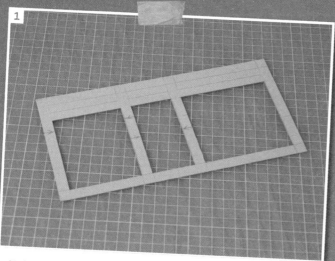

1

Make a template out of greyboard to use as a stencil. Use the outer measurements of the piece and include all the gaps you plan to cut. Use this stencil to draw the pattern on each base piece, numbering the pieces as you go to help maintain the design.

2

Cut out each base and the appropriate gaps. Glue the bases to each other according to the numbered order.

DESKTOP ORGANIZER

A desk should be a convenient workspace as well as a place to store things. However, with the amount of paper, receipts, pens, cords, books, cards, binders, paper clips, coffee mugs and dirty dishes most of us accumulate, there's often not enough room for a Post-It® note, let alone a computer monitor and a keyboard.

So what do you do? Build a desktop organizer! In the following piece we tried to make sure that there would be shelves for your papers, upright compartments for your files, and a drawer for any random junk you may want to keep around. These instructions should only serve as inspiration, though—feel free to fit the organizer to your needs! Any random object that fits can be used as a drawer pull; we used an old stereo volume button. Turn to page 16 ("Found Objects") if you need more inspiration.

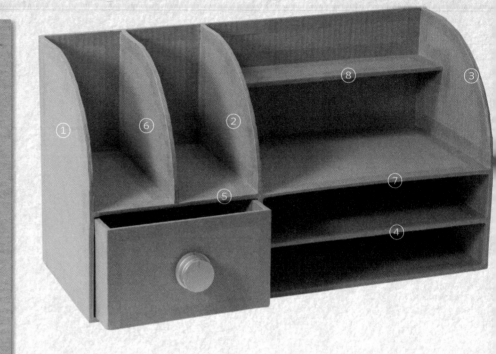

KEEP READING FOR MORE!

MATERIAL & TOOLS

- ☐ Corrugated cardboard (2.5mm)
- ☐ Handle for the drawer
- ☐ Kraft tape

- ☐ Craft knife
- ☐ Ruler
- ☐ Triangle protractor
- ☐ Compass
- ☐ Pencil

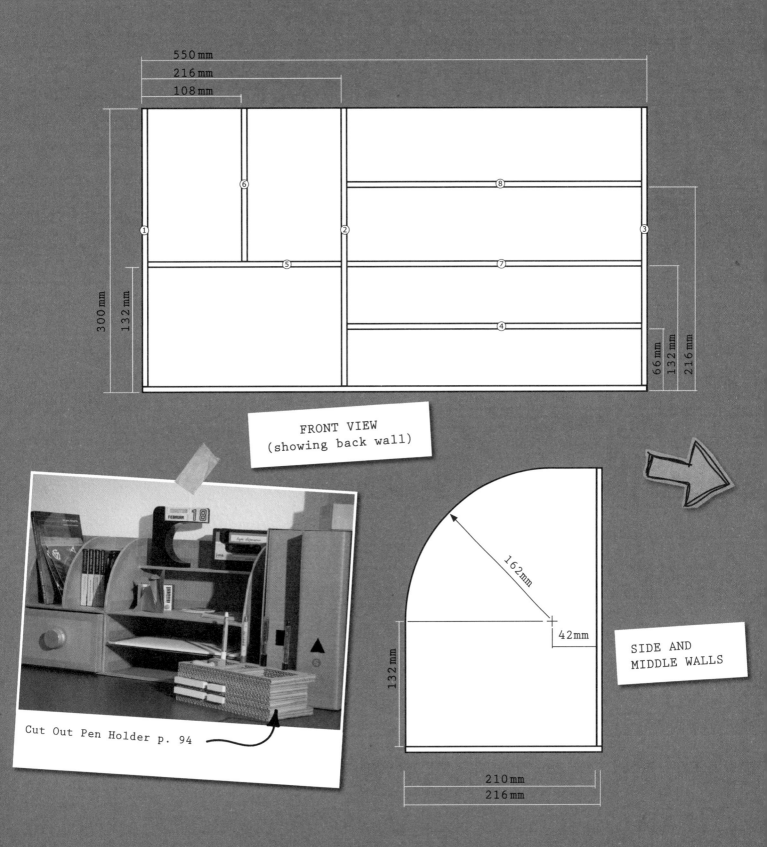

550 mm

216 mm

108 mm

300 mm

132 mm

⑥ ① ② ③ ④ ⑤ ⑦ ⑧

66 mm

132 mm

216 mm

FRONT VIEW
(showing back wall)

Cut Out Pen Holder p. 94

162 mm

42 mm

132 mm

210 mm

216 mm

SIDE AND
MIDDLE WALLS

Construction:

1. Cut the side (① & ③), middle (②) and back panels and base).

2. Mark where panel numbers ④ ⑤ ⑥ and ⑧ will be positioned on the walls so later you can see where to attach them.

3. Attach the sides, middle panels, back and base.

4. Attach piece ④.

5. Attach piece ⑤ and ⑥.

6. Attach piece ⑦ and ⑧.

7. Seal the end walls with kraft tape.

8. The drawer is built exactly like a simple square box (page 58). It's wise to first assemble the desktop organizer, then carefully measure the inner dimensions of the drawer gap to make sure the drawer will fit precisely. Draw the drawer plan so that the outer measurements are all 2mm smaller than the drawer gap. This will ensure that the drawer fits well and doesn't get stuck in the organizer.

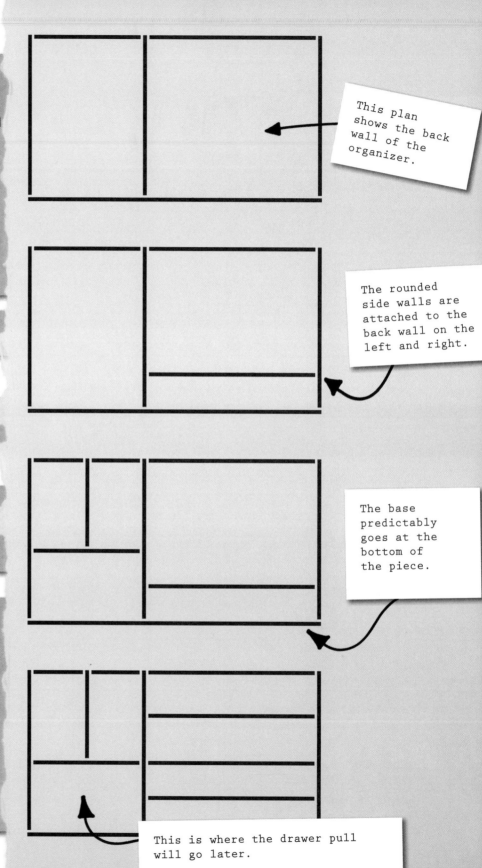

This plan shows the back wall of the organizer.

The rounded side walls are attached to the back wall on the left and right.

The base predictably goes at the bottom of the piece.

This is where the drawer pull will go later.

Attaching the drawer pull:

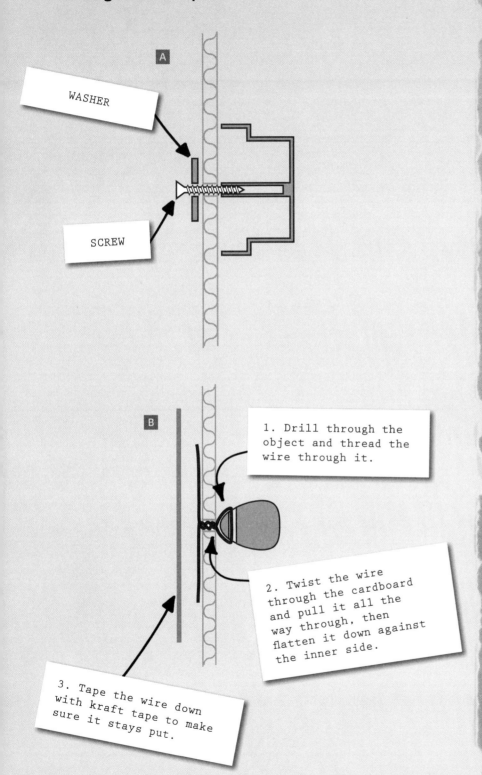

WASHER

SCREW

A

1. Drill through the object and thread the wire through it.

2. Twist the wire through the cardboard and pull it all the way through, then flatten it down against the inner side.

3. Tape the wire down with kraft tape to make sure it stays put.

B

There are many ways to attach the drawer pull depending on the object you're using. There are three standard methods:

A The knobs on a stereo system have a hole in the center for the pin that turns the controls. It's possible to drill a suitably-sized screw into this hole, then attach it to the outside of the drawer with a hot glue gun. A washer should be placed between the head of the screw and the inside of the cardboard to make sure the screw won't be torn out through the cardboard. You can attach anything you can drill a hole into using this method.

B Items with pre-drilled holes, like buttons or wooden beads, can be attached with a piece of wire. Thread the wire through the hole, making sure both ends are equal in length, and fix it in place by twisting it around two or three times. The wire ends are then threaded through the cardboard and bent against the inside. Use a piece of kraft tape or other tape to keep them in place.

C If you have a knob with a larger surface area, you can simply glue it on. Don't trust hot glue for this—super glue or Epoxy resin will give you a solid, durable connection.

"LEPORELLO" NOTICE BOARD

The "Leporello" board gives you an elegant opportunity to save and show your favorite photos, postcards and flyers without damaging them. The name refers to the accordion-like folds of the surface (also known as pleats) that form pockets in which one can store flat objects.

The pattern provided shows where to make mountain and valley folds at regular intervals. You can use basically any material with the right measurements that can be precisely folded. In our experience, material with a width of 70cm and a paper weight of 110 to 140lb card stock is most suitable. Below that weight the pleats are unstable, and above it the material breaks when folded.

You can use a variety of different materials with the Leporello to achieve different looks, such as posters or bright wallpaper. If your pictures are bright enough on their own and you'd like a neutral Leporello, use black photo backing paper like we did in our example.

MATERIALS & TOOLS

- ☐ Large format stiff paper (such as 110lb cardstock). For example, a poster, photo backing paper, etc.
- ☐ An old picture frame: you will need one without glass, but that still has its back.

- ☐ Bone folder
- ☐ Craft knife
- ☐ Long ruler (for extra lengths you could use a wallpaper cutting guide)
- ☐ Pencil
- ☐ Cutting matt or other soft base for folding.
- ☐ Tape
- ☐ Another person for a helping hand.

KEEP GOING FOR CONSTRUCTION INSTRUCTIONS!

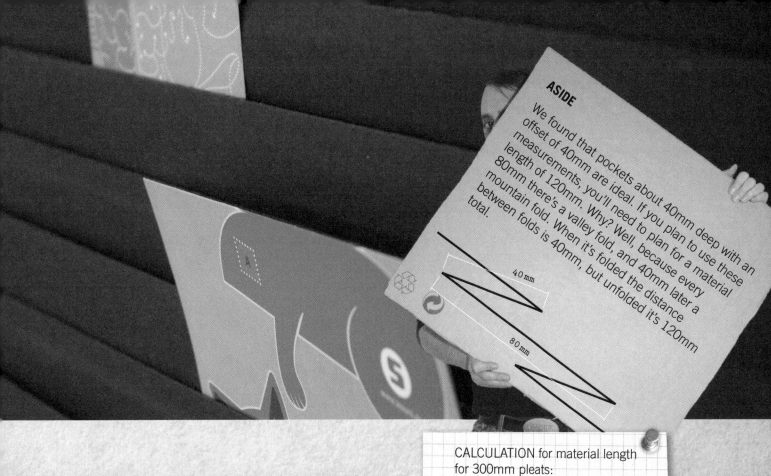

CALCULATION for material length for 300mm pleats:

300 : 40 = 7.5

7.5 x 120 = 900 mm

With so many long folds, it's nearly impossible to work toward an exact measurement. Save yourself from stress and pick a length of material that is 10 or 15 cm longer than the inner measurements of your frame. Another good general rule is to add 10% of the required width to your material. This way you can relax while making your pleats and don't have to worry about keeping all of the folds exactly parallel. When you reach your desired height, just cut the pleats to the right width and fix the piece to the picture frame.

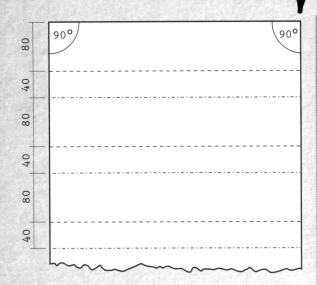

END WALL

90°　　　　　　　90°

80
40
80
40
80
40

TIP

Don't remember what these different dashed lines mean? Check page 19!

Construction:

1 First measure the inside of the picture frame you're going to insert your folded paper into.

2 If you already know what you want to put on the board, try laying it all out to help you decide if it will look better vertically or horizontally.

3 Determine the format of the folds and the amount of material you'll need. For 300mm pleats you'll need approximately 900mm of material. If the material you have doesn't fit the format, you can adjust the size of the pockets.

4 Draw on the measurements. Make sure the material is the required width and that the edges are parallel; this will ensure that they'll fit into the frame later on. The end should be cut at a 90° angle so it can serve as a reference line for your folds.

5 Draw on the guidelines for the folds. Use double folds if the width of the material allows for it. To do this, use the craft knife to lightly cut through the markings at notable spots. If your format is too big and you must do single folds, you can use a pencil to draw out the measurements. Mark the front and the back side of the material you'll be folding.

6 Follow the markings to fold the material into mountain and valley folds. Your trusty bone folder will help you here. It might also be useful to have someone hold the ruler for you when you're dealing with large lengths of material.

7 If you need to, fix the pleats in place on the back using strips of adhesive tape.

8 Make sure the last edge of the material is straight. The back wall of the frame can help you here.

9 Attach the pleated material to the back piece of the picture frame using double-sided tape, then attach the back and the pleats to the frame itself. Mount the frame on the wall and begin the best part: arranging your keepsakes on your new notice board.

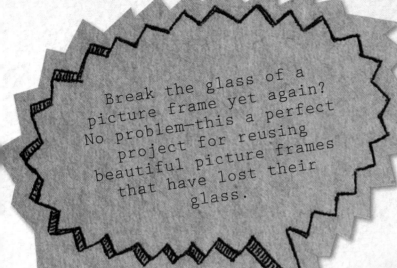

Break the glass of a picture frame yet again? No problem—this a perfect project for reusing beautiful picture frames that have lost their glass.

VARIATIONS

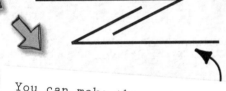

You can make the pockets deeper if you need to accommodate different sizes or formats.

It only begins with postcards and photos! The variable nature of our notice board means that it can be beautifully turned into any sort of calendar, from a birthday board to an advent calendar or weekly planner. It could even be turned into creative learning tool with the right organization.

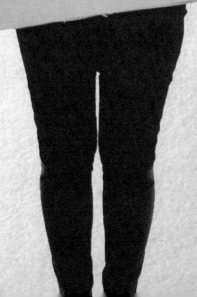

The finished pleats will have an incredible amount of tension in them. If you're worried about them staying folded, you can always stick the individual folds together on the back using adhesive tape. If you do this, make sure that the pleats are lying flat on the work surface or are pressed flat with a ruler or another tool.

Because of the tension in the pleats, you'll need to be able to securely attach the back piece to the front of the picture frame, and make sure it is stable when you hang it. Nails or picture hooks are recommended, as are picture frames with bendable metal fixtures.

WALL ORGANIZER

Chaos on your desktop? Can't get to your drawers? Losing all of your tools? Prepare to put these problems behind you—the time has come for this fantastic and practical wall organizer!

Using the skills you learned in the box chapter, you can design and build a wall organizer to precisely suit your own tastes.

MATERIALS & TOOLS

- ☐ A large piece of cardboard for the back wall (6mm)
- ☐ Cardboard for the compart-ments (2.5–6mm)

- ☐ Craft knife
- ☐ Ruler
- ☐ Triangle protractor
- ☐ Pencil
- ☐ Kraft tape

All of your supplies at your service!

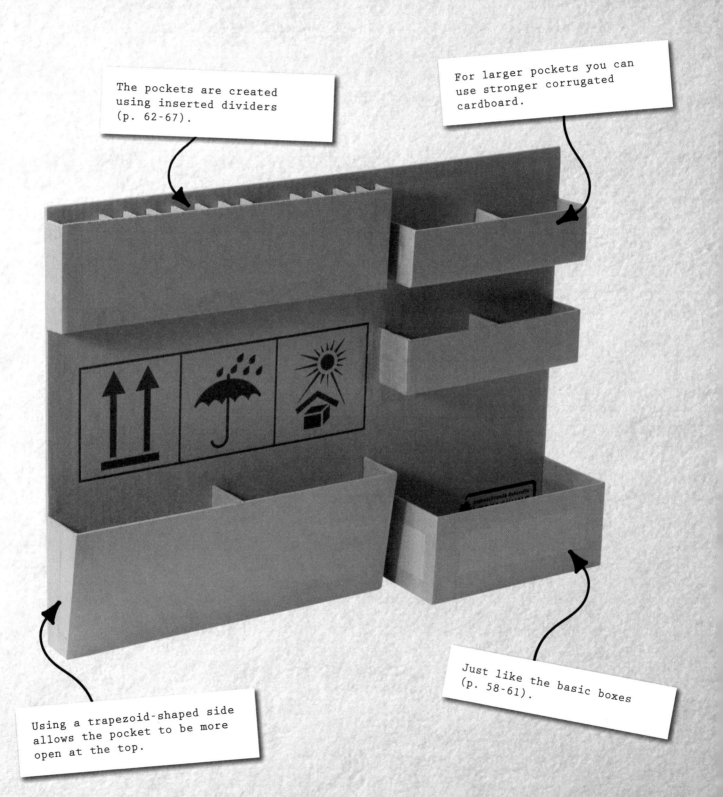

The pockets are created using inserted dividers (p. 62-67).

For larger pockets you can use stronger corrugated cardboard.

Using a trapezoid-shaped side allows the pocket to be more open at the top.

Just like the basic boxes (p. 58-61).

MAGAZINE FILE BOX

This magazine file box keeps your projects organized until they're finished. It will patiently accept newspaper clippings, writing pads, diaries and loose sheets. It's highly practical and has a calming effect on stressed eyes.

Our guide is only an example of what this project can look like. It's easy to customize it to fit your needs! Two boxes, five boxes—no problem. The only restriction is that if you want to store files and print-outs, be sure that the dividers can accommodate 8 1/2" x 11" paper.

You'll notice in the images that the front of our boxes are folded rather than cut. We found this fold already made in some packaging material, and its measurements fit exactly. This is great example of how you can get lucky with your cardboard projects! Of course, we'll still show how these are built from individual pieces in the instructions.

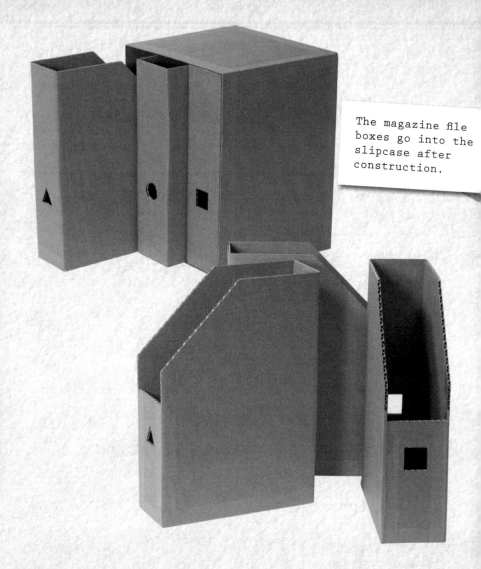

The magazine file boxes go into the slipcase after construction.

MATERIALS & TOOLS

- [ ] Corrugated cardboard (2.5mm)

- [ ] Craft knife
- [ ] Ruler
- [ ] Triangle protractor
- [ ] Pencil
- [ ] Kraft tape

Construction:

1 Draw and cut out the parts for as many file boxes as you'd like to make.

2 Assemble the file boxes. They're built just like the square box: the sides are mounted directly on to the base, and the longer side walls extend to enclose the front and back pieces.

3 Draw the pieces for the slipcase and cut it out. The slipcase is also assembled like the basic square box. The back of the slipcase corresponds to the base of a basic box.

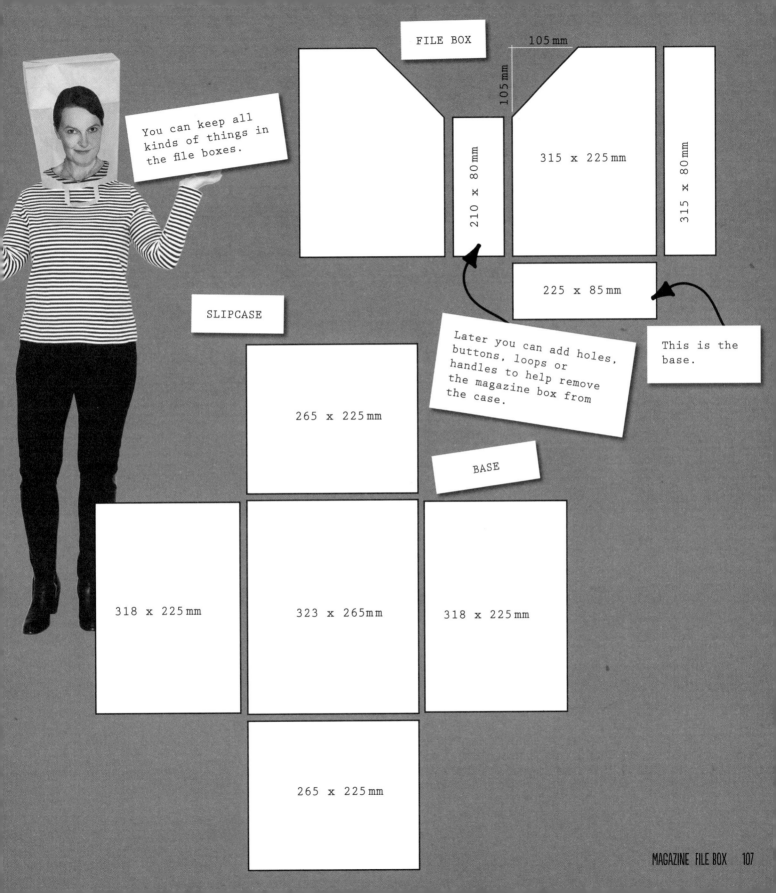

FILE BOX

105 mm

105 mm

210 x 80 mm

315 x 225 mm

315 x 80 mm

You can keep all kinds of things in the file boxes.

225 x 85 mm

SLIPCASE

265 x 225 mm

Later you can add holes, buttons, loops or handles to help remove the magazine box from the case.

This is the base.

BASE

318 x 225 mm

323 x 265 mm

318 x 225 mm

265 x 225 mm

OFFICE "ACTION" BOX

The office action box emerged during a moment of need in our office. Imagine this scenario: A complex craft project, a tiny workspace, tools and scraps everywhere...basically, the best way to make sure you can't find anything you need when you need it.

Simply stick the tools you know you'll need upright in the office box and they'll be well-organized and easy to find. When you're done with them, organize them in the large compartments, close the lid, and your work is done!

Design the arrangement of the inner pockets to suit your own needs.

LOTS OF POCKETS FOR PENS!

MATERIAL & TOOLS

- ☐ Corrugated cardboard (6mm)

- ☐ Craft knife
- ☐ Ruler
- ☐ Triangle protractor
- ☐ Pencil
- ☐ Kraft tape

Construction:

1. Cut all the parts for the box and the lid from the corrugated cardboard.

2. Assemble the box and lid and attach them with kraft tape.

3. Plan the layout of the inner compartments.

4. Cut and insert your dividers. Check page 62 ("With Compartments") if you need a reminder on how to do this.

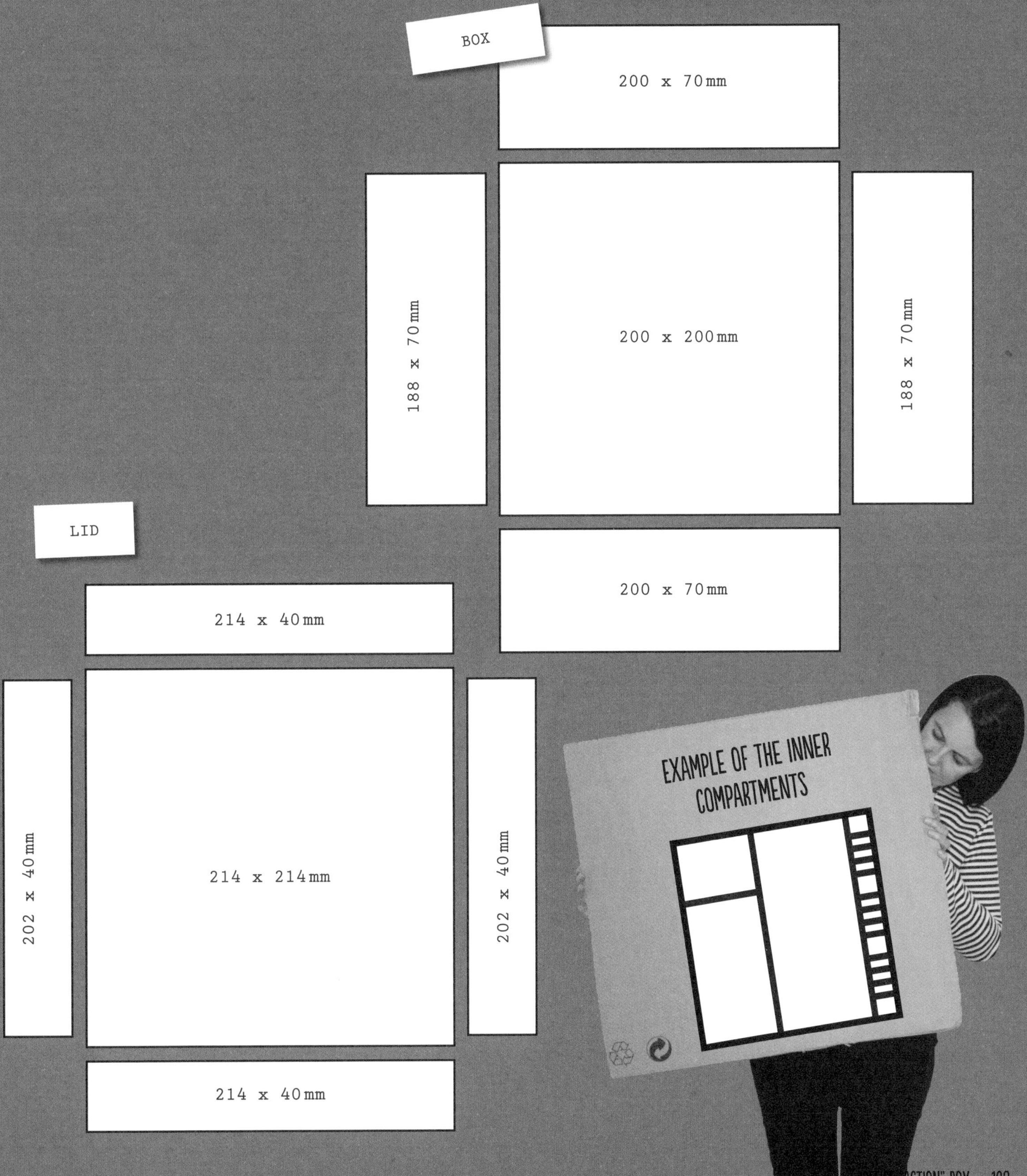

200 x 70mm

188 x 70mm

200 x 200mm

188 x 70mm

200 x 70mm

LID

214 x 40mm

202 x 40mm

214 x 214mm

202 x 40mm

214 x 40mm

EXAMPLE OF THE INNER COMPARTMENTS

SORTING BOX WITH HINGE

The sorting box complements the office action box. Here, too, you can tailor the inner compartments to suit your needs.

MATERIAL & TOOLS

- ☐ Corrugated cardboard (6mm)

- ☐ Craft knife
- ☐ Ruler
- ☐ Triangle protractor
- ☐ Pencil
- ☐ Kraft tape

Construction:

1 Cut out the pieces for the box and lid from corrugated cardboard.

2 Assemble the box and lid separately with kraft tape.

3 Cut the compartments you want and insert them. Refer to page 62 "With Compartments" if needed.

4 Attach the lid and box to each other, using kraft tape as a hinge (see page 72 "With Hinges").

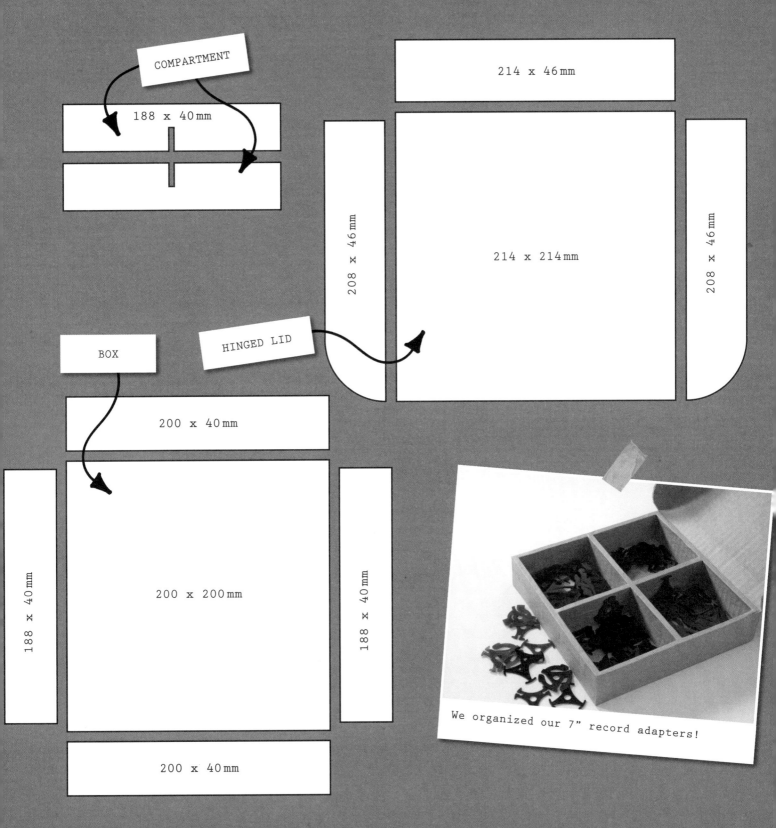

COMPARTMENT

188 x 40mm

214 x 46mm

208 x 46mm

214 x 214mm

208 x 46mm

BOX

HINGED LID

200 x 40mm

188 x 40mm

200 x 200mm

188 x 40mm

200 x 40mm

We organized our 7" record adapters!

LAPTOP STAND

This laptop stand will raise your monitor to a more ergonomic height and save you space on your desk: first, with the smaller amount of room your laptop takes up, and second, by giving you an extra space for storage. It has room for loose cords, flash drives, and whatever else you might want close at hand.

These measurements are intended for a 15" laptop. If you have a smaller laptop, build a stand that is narrower and shorter to match your laptop's size.

MATERIAL & TOOLS

- ☐ Corrugated cardboard (6mm) for the walls
- ☐ Corrugated cardboard (2.5mm) for the base/back wall and aperture/front

- ☐ Craft knife
- ☐ Ruler
- ☐ Triangle protractor
- ☐ Bone folder
- ☐ Pencil
- ☐ Kraft tape

No more back pain—thank you, laptop stand!

Construction:

1. Draw the sidepieces on sturdy 6mm corrugated cardboard and cut them out.

2. Draw the base/back wall and lip on corrugated cardboard. Don't forget to draw your top and bottom edges perpendicular to the corrugation!

3. Mount and attach the side parts to the base and back wall. Attach the middle piece.

4. Finally, attach the front lip.

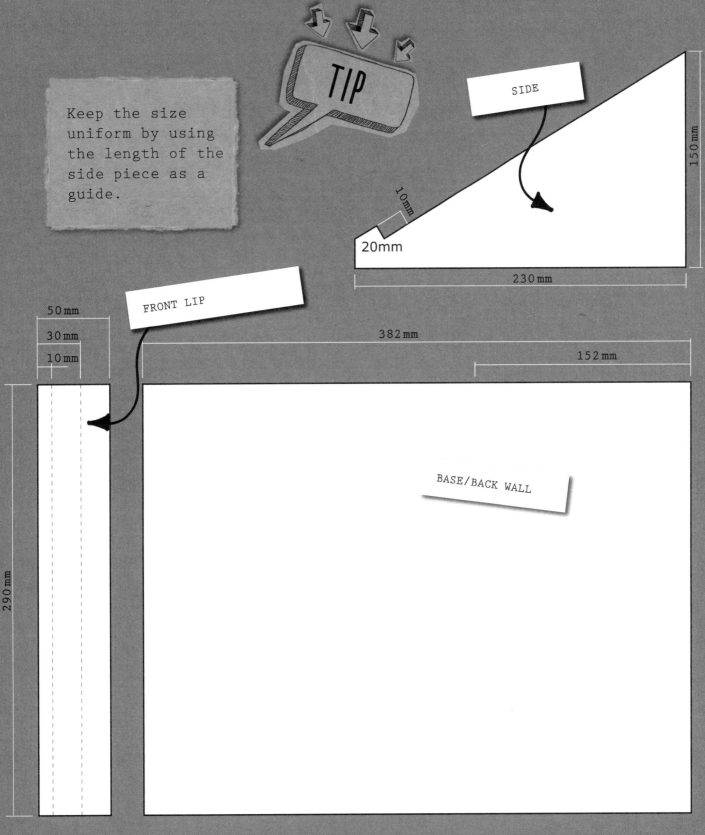

TAPE DISPENSER

The most important material in this book after cardboard is—anyone? Anyone? Correct! It's tape! While kraft tape often has a small hole in the center (or no hole at all), many large rolls of tape have an open center. We discovered something interesting—most of these big rolls will fit nicely over a tin can, a perfect arrangement for a home-made tape dispenser.

Except for the inward-facing lip in the front, the tape dispenser is just a basic box. The tin can sits in a groove on each side.

MATERIAL & TOOLS

- ☐ Corrugated cardboard (6mm)
- ☐ Small tin can (75 x 110mm)

- ☐ Craft knife
- ☐ Ruler
- ☐ Triangle protractor
- ☐ Pencil
- ☐ Compass
- ☐ Kraft tape

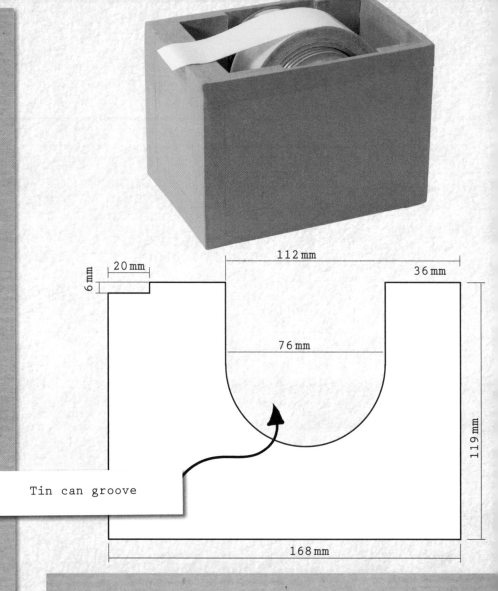

Tin can groove

Construction:

1 Draw and cut the pieces for the basic box. Assemble everything except for the inward-facing lip.

2 Draw and cut out the grooves for the tin can.

3 Fit the inside pieces with the grooves into the box.

4 Attach the inward-facing lip in the front of the box.

5 Finish by covering cut edges with kraft tape.

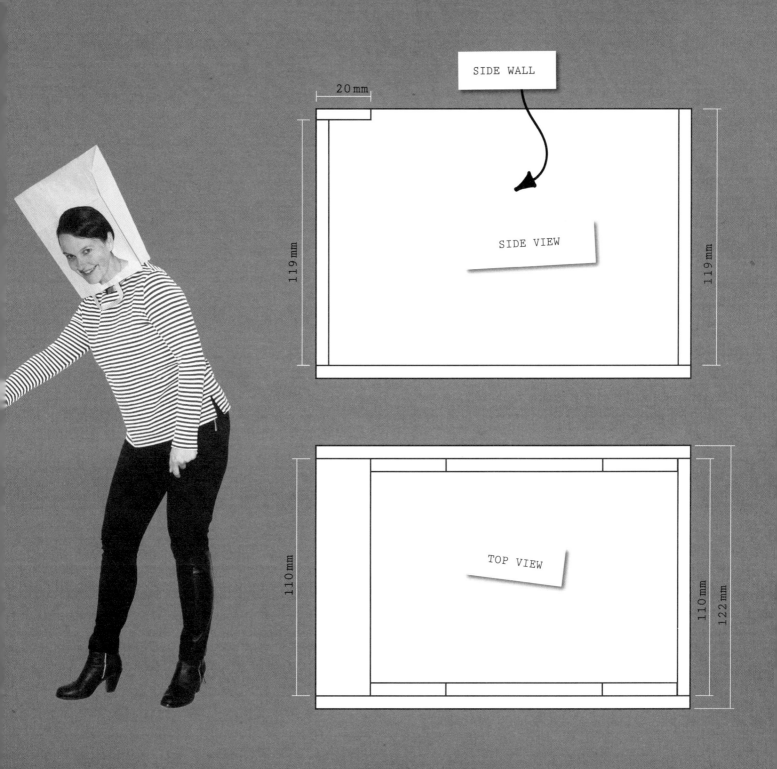

20 mm

SIDE WALL

119 mm

SIDE VIEW

119 mm

110 mm

TOP VIEW

110 mm

122 mm

MULTIFACETED WASTEBASKET

Building a wastebasket out of waste is the ultimate form of recycling! It's a bit like sausage: You stuff all the unwanted leftover scraps into the casing, and—er, maybe we should find a different analogy…

In any case, here's a multifaceted wastebasket with a wide mouth for catching all sort of office waste.

MATERIAL & TOOLS

- ☐ Corrugated cardboard (6mm)

- ☐ Craft knife
- ☐ Ruler
- ☐ Triangle protractor
- ☐ Pencil
- ☐ Kraft tape

Construction:

1 Draw and cut five copies of each piece, excluding the base.

2 Flip pieces ②, ③ and ④ so that the underside of the cardboard is facing up. With kraft tape, attach the pieces so they lay flat and flush against each other (Fig. 1).

3 Attach all of the assembled sides to the underside of the base (Fig. 2).

4 Stand the pieces upright and tape pieces ③ and ④ together on the inside. Be careful, the basket still isn't stable!

5 Attach piece ① to the top of piece ③ from the inside.

6 Attach pieces ① and ② together from the inside. This will give the wastebasket more stability.

7 Go over all the joints on the outside with kraft tape.

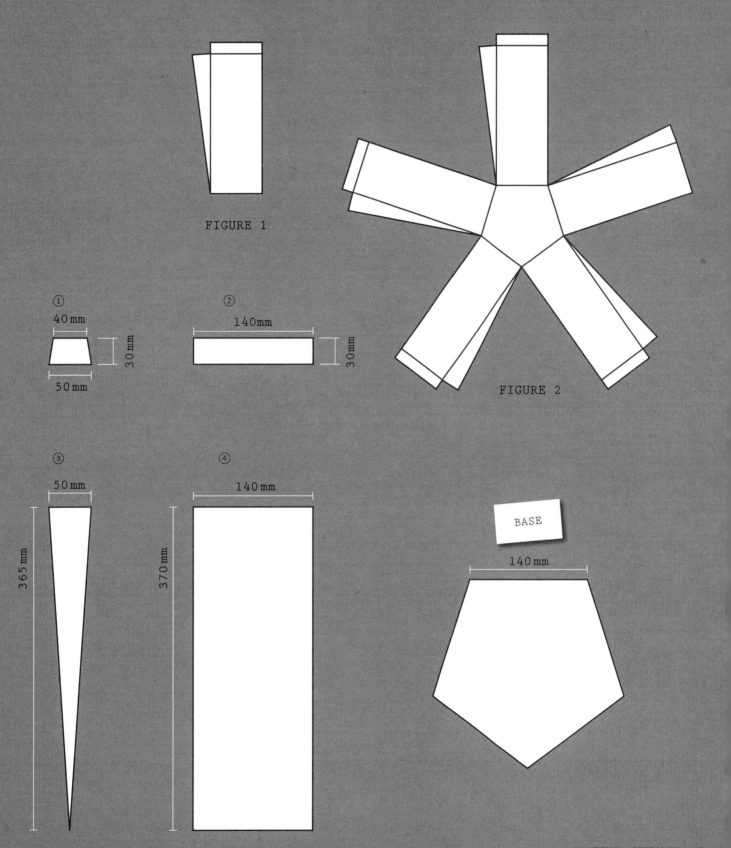

FIGURE 1

① 40 mm
50 mm
30 mm

② 140mm
30mm

FIGURE 2

③ 50 mm
365 mm

④ 140 mm
370 mm

BASE
140 mm

ORGANIZING INSERTS FOR DRAWERS

The time is up for drawers overflowing with junk! These individual inserts are quick to make, will fit any drawer, and can organize even the strangest of drawer debris. Your neat drawers will satisfy even the most finicky of mother-in-laws.

These inserts make finding things in your drawers a breeze!

MATERIAL & TOOLS

☐ Corrugated cardboard (6mm)

☐ Craft knife
☐ Ruler
☐ Triangle profractor
☐ Pencil
☐ Kraft tape

Construction:

1. Measure the drawer before you start so you'll be sure your organizer will fit. Plan out the divisions you want.

2. Cut strips of cardboard that are the same height as the inner depth of the drawer.

3. Make slotted joints to connect the long pieces to each other. Fix the inner corners using folded kraft tape.

4. Cut the short dividers and attach them securely.

5. It's up to you whether or not to cover the upper edge of the divider with kraft tape.

CORRUGATED CARDBOARD
DIVIDER FOR INSERTION

SHORT DIVIDER

TAPING
INSTRUCTIONS
ON PAGE 26

You can never have too many rulers!

CHAPTER 5

SHELVES

FREESTANDING SHELF

Have you found a beautiful box that you just can't bring yourself to cut into? You can always leave it as-is and make a freestanding shelf out of it! You can make a shelf for your desk from smaller boxes—large boxes can be made into bookshelves, a cabinet for your stereo, or even a wardrobe by attaching doors or a curtain.

MATERIAL & TOOLS

☐ Sturdy, wide box (corrugated cardboard 4-6mm)

☐ Craft knife
☐ Ruler
☐ Triangle Protractor
☐ Pencil
☐ Kraft Tape
☐ Hot glue gun (if necessary)

Construction:

1 If your box is too deep, you can cut it to a new depth. Just draw a line at the desired depth on the outside of the box and make a new fold for the lid.

2 Mark the depth of the box minus 2-3mm on all four of the top flaps and shorten them to fit. They'll be folded into the box later to provide more stability for the shelves, so be sure these cuts are accurate.

3 Put the box on its side. Draw and cut slits equal to the thickness of the material in the top flaps for the shelves (Fig. 2), as well as slits for the stabilizing strips (page 124, Fig. 3).

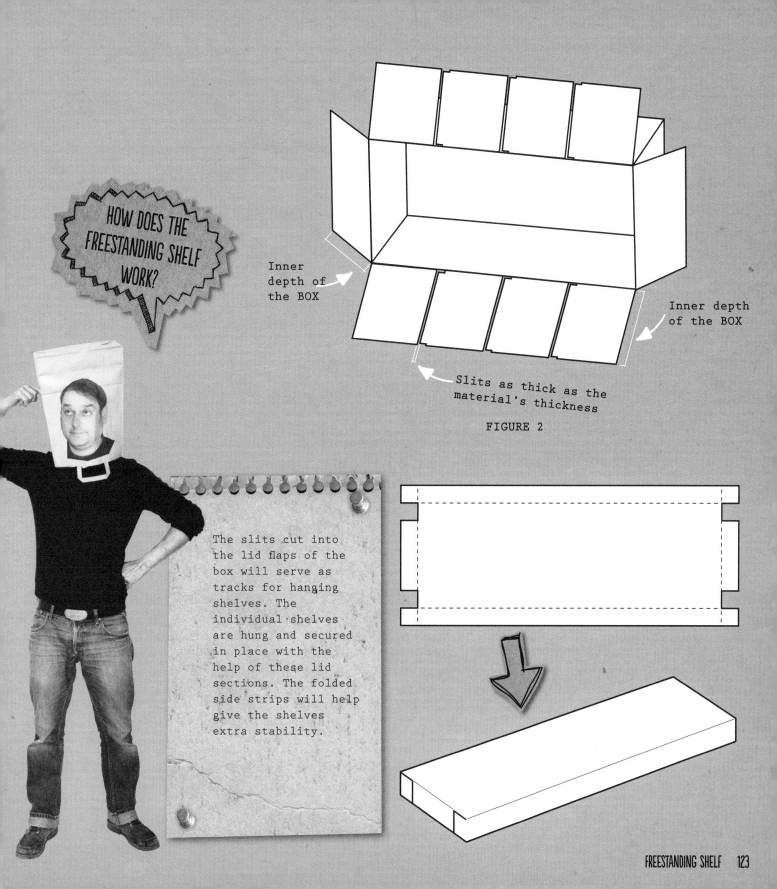

Inner
depth of
the BOX

Inner depth
of the BOX

Slits as thick as the
material's thickness

FIGURE 2

HOW DOES THE
FREESTANDING SHELF
WORK?

The slits cut into
the lid flaps of the
box will serve as
tracks for hanging
shelves. The
individual shelves
are hung and secured
in place with the
help of these lid
sections. The folded
side strips will help
give the shelves
extra stability.

4 Now draw the shelves. The outside measurement of the shelf corresponds to the inner measurement of the box (width and depth). The stabilizing strips go all the way around each shelf and should be 3-5cm wide. The larger the stabilizing strip, the more stable the shelf. Strips 2cm wide are fine for narrow shelves 20cm wide or smaller. Draw two square gaps in the strip at each end of the shelf; the flaps of the long sides of the strips will fit in these. Finally, cut and fold the whole thing (Fig. 3).

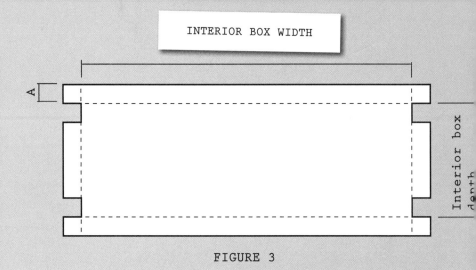

INTERIOR BOX WIDTH

A

Interior box depth

FIGURE 3

5 Fold the flaps on the bottom of the shelf into the box. If they're too tight, trim just a few millimeters off the bottom of the flaps, based on the thickness of the material. Next, fold the bottom lid flap into the box, trimming it slightly if it's too tight. The bottom flap will help hold the side flaps in position.

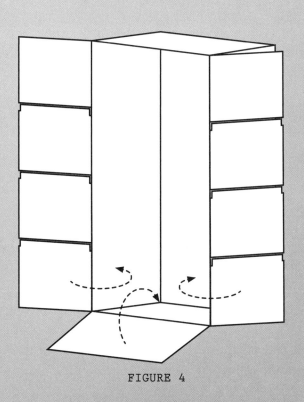

FIGURE 4

FIGURE 5

6 Fold the shelf and insert it carefully into the slits between the side flaps. Work your way up from the bottom, folding flaps and inserting shelves as you go (Fig. 5).

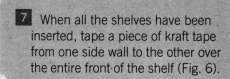

7 When all the shelves have been inserted, tape a piece of kraft tape from one side wall to the other over the entire front of the shelf (Fig. 6).

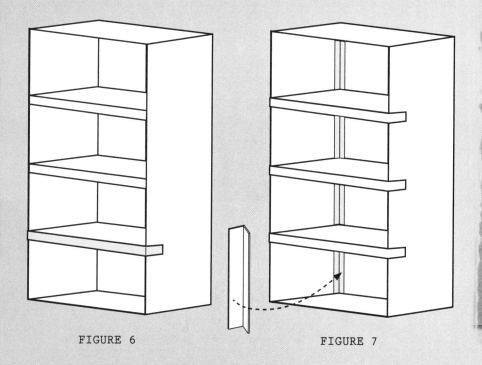

FIGURE 6   FIGURE 7

8 If the lid flaps won't stay in place, you'll need to fix them down. One way to do this is to use double-sided masking tap on the inside between the inside wall and the flap; another solution is to make corner inserts that can be hot glued or taped into position to help keep the side flap folded tightly against the walls (Fig. 7).

SIMPLE WALL SHELF

You may be wondering why this project is called the "simple wall shelf" when the instructions, with all those lines and circles, seem incredibly complicated. Once you understand the principle, though, you'll smack your forehead and cry, "Man, the whole thing really is simple!" There's another reason for the title, too: this shelf is made from one closed body that gains stability from its own construction, like half a pyramid. The shelf can also be hung on the wall as soon as you're finished building it. Super simple!

MATERIAL & TOOLS

- ☐ Corrugated cardboard (2.5mm)

- ☐ Craft knife
- ☐ Ruler
- ☐ Pencil
- ☐ Triangle protractor
- ☐ Compass
- ☐ Kraft tape

Diamonds for your walls.

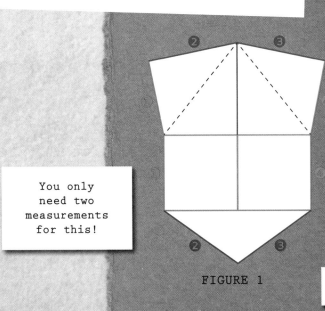

You only need two measurements for this!

FIGURE 1

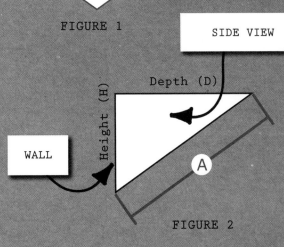

SIDE VIEW

Depth (D)

Height (H)

WALL

A

FIGURE 2

How does the simple shelf work?

How does the simple shelf work? Well, the basic principle of the shelf is very simple: The entire piece is made with only three measurements. Two of them you set yourself; the third will evolve during the drawing process.

The outline starts with two measurements. The drawing shows which sides will be attached after it is cut out.

We'll show you a simple way to build this piece without much math. To keep things simple we recommend the following ratio:

Depth (D) = 1

Width (W) = 2

Height (H) = 2/3 of the Depth

(this will eventually be rounded)

The advantage of using this ratio is that you can just measure the length (A) of the front side of the shelf in your drawing without having to calculate it. This only works with equation D x W = 1 x 2, ensuring that the piece is twice as wide as it is deep. On the right you'll find a tip for calculating your own dimensions.

Check Figures 2 and 3 for the arrangement of depth/width/height.

Our measurements for the example ratio are:

Depth (D) = 150mm

Width (W) = 300mm

Height (H) = 100mm

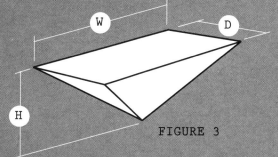

FIGURE 3

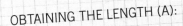

OBTAINING THE LENGTH (A):

There are two ways you can obtain the length of the front piece (A):

1. Draw two lines at 90°angles the length of the intended height and depth of the shelf, and measure the length (A) between the endpoints of the two lines.

2. Use the Pythagorean Theorem ($a^2+b^2=c^2$), where the depth (D) and the rear side (height, H) of the shelf are at right angles.

EXAMPLE:

Depth: 150mm

Height: 100mm

$150^2 + 100^2 = 22,500 + 10,000 = 32,500$ = Front measurement squared

$\sqrt{32,500} = 180.27$ mm = Length A

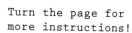

Turn the page for more instructions!

Here's how to build the shelf using our measurements:

1 Find a piece of 2.5mm corrugated cardboard that measures approximately 650 x 550mm (H x W), so you have extra room to draw on it.

2 Draw your center line on the inner side of the cardboard parallel to the width, leaving approximately 150mm to the left and right of the line (Illustration 1).

3 Draw the height at 90° to the center line and connect the points so they form a triangle (Illustration 2).

4 Draw the depth line (upper side) parallel to the height line (Illustration 3).

5 Set your compass to length "A" (here, 180.2mm). Place the point of the compass at the intersection of the depth line and the center line and draw half a circle above the depth line (Illustration 4).

6 Draw a circle, using the intersection of your arc and the center line as the center point of the circle (Illustration 5).

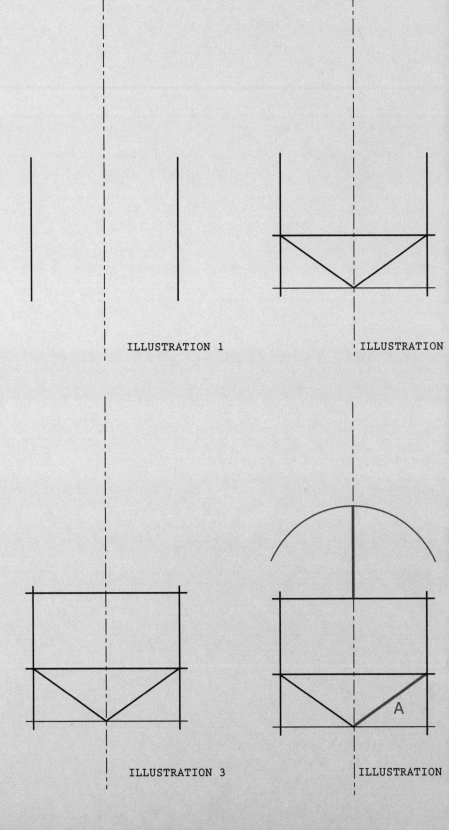

ILLUSTRATION 1

ILLUSTRATION

ILLUSTRATION 3

ILLUSTRATION

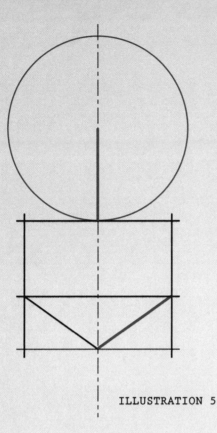

ILLUSTRATION 5

7 Set the compass to length "D" (the depth of your shelf) and draw two circles, each centered on the point where your 150mm measurement on each side of the center line and the depth line intersect. Draw a line from the center of these circles to the center of the larger circle. These lines mark the inside edges of the side pieces (Illustration 6).

8 Fold along the dashed lines and cut along the outline you drew.

9 Fold the shelf (with the drawing inside) and close the open edges with kraft tape.

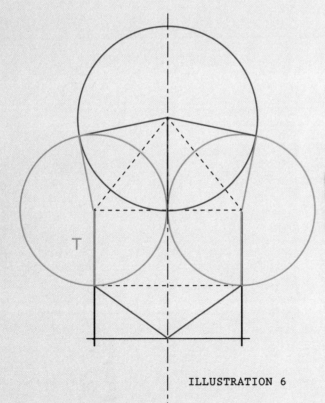

ILLUSTRATION 6

TIP

We recommend using nails or picture hooks to hang these shelves. Poke two through the back side and hang the shelf from them, making sure it's level.

WEDGE WALL SHELF

The construction of this shelf is totally freestyle. You can design it entirely to fit your own needs and desires.

For the shelf in the picture we experimented with wedges 200 to 350mm wide, 120 to 200mm high and 150 to 300mm deep. The shelf is built like a basic box, but with only one short side wall.

MATERIALS & TOOLS

☐ Corrugated cardboard (6mm)

☐ Craft cutter
☐ Ruler
☐ Triangle protractor
☐ Pencil
☐ Kraft tape

Hang more shelves above and below…

…to accommodate all of your sweet rides.

BACK PIECE
(the base
during
construction)

CHAPTER 6

LAMPS

SAFETY!

All of the lampshades shown here are intended to be used only with LED or energy saver light bulbs. Conventional bulbs or halogen lights emit too much heat, and using them could result in fire!

These projects are meant as lampshades only. Make sure lamps are turned off or unplugged before you attempt to attach them, and do not place them directly on to light bulbs! Please remember to always use caution when working near electricity.

"PLANES" LAMP

This lamp's most important feature is that it's held together by slotted joints. The outer frames of the lampshade are 24 individual frames that are assembled to form 12 pieces that can then be slotted into place.

MATERIALS & TOOLS

- ☐ Corrugated cardboard (2.5mm)
- ☐ Tracing or tissue paper
- ☐ Standard light fixture
- ☐ Standard size lightbulb (LED or energy saver)

- ☐ Craft knife
- ☐ Ruler
- ☐ Triangle protractor
- ☐ Pencil
- ☐ PVA Glue

A variation with original artwork.

VARIATIONS

You can build on the construction principle of this project (the slotted joints) to create a variety of different forms and projects. The inserted pieces and cutouts don't have to be squares. Try this project with circles, rectangles or free-form shapes. The same applies to choosing the material for filling the frames. White tracing paper is neutral, but you can partially tint the light by using red or yellow tissue paper. Green and blue are good if you like cooler shades. Try using foreign language newspapers for an international feel. A nice touch for a child's bedroom is to let them draw the insertions themselves with a felt-tipped pen. A wonderful side effect of using transparent paper is that you can use it to trace all sorts of images for your own use.

When constructing your own creations, it may be helpful use the connectors (components ① & ②) we show for "Planes," but you can also insert the frames directly into each other.

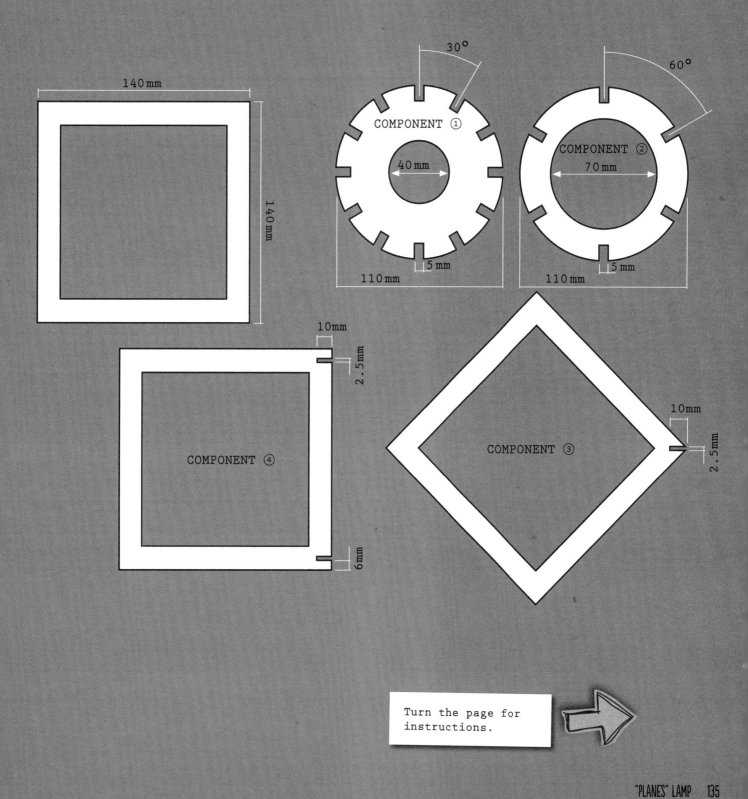

140 mm

140 mm

30°

COMPONENT ①

40 mm

110 mm

5 mm

60°

COMPONENT ②

70 mm

110 mm

5 mm

10mm

2.5 mm

COMPONENT ④

6 mm

COMPONENT ③

10mm

2.5 mm

Turn the page for
instructions.

TIP

If needed, you can roll up a piece of transparent paper (125 wide x 220mm long) to place between components 1 and 2. The tension from the two components will keep the paper in place behind the protrusions.

Construction:

1. Cut 24 140 x 140mm frames.

2. Sandwich a piece of tracing paper or tissue paper between two frames.

3. Draw components ① and ② and cut them out.

4. Slot the frames into the appropriate slits on the circular components. There will be six pieces each of components ③ and ④.

5. Attach component ① to the lamp.

COMPONENT ①

COMPONENT ③

COMPONENT ④

COMPONENT ②

Connect components ③ and ④ to component ① alternating their order all the way around the piece.

Fit component ③ into the lower slots of component ②

TIP

Test the slotted joints with spare bits of cardboard before you cut out your frames. The slots should be slightly smaller than the thickness of the frame, so the material is held tightly and the components are well-connected.

LARGE DIAMOND LAMP

The large diamond lamp looks great above a dining table. The larger you make the measurements of components ① and ② marked in blue on the opposite page, the flatter and wider the lamp will be.

MATERIALS & TOOLS

- ☐ Corrugated cardboard (2.5mm)
- ☐ Standard size light fixture
- ☐ Standard size lightbulb (LED or energy saver)

- ☐ Craft knife
- ☐ Ruler
- ☐ Triangle Protractor
- ☐ Pencil
- ☐ Kraft tape

Acute angles will make steeper sides.

Construction:

1. Draw each component six times and cut them all out.

2. Lay the parts out as shown in Figure 1, with the back side of the cardboard facing up and the connecting edges facing outward. Attach everything with kraft tape.

3. Tape the two outer edges of component ① together.

4. Attach component ① to componenet ② with kraft tape.

5. Cover the flaps from the outside with kraft tape.

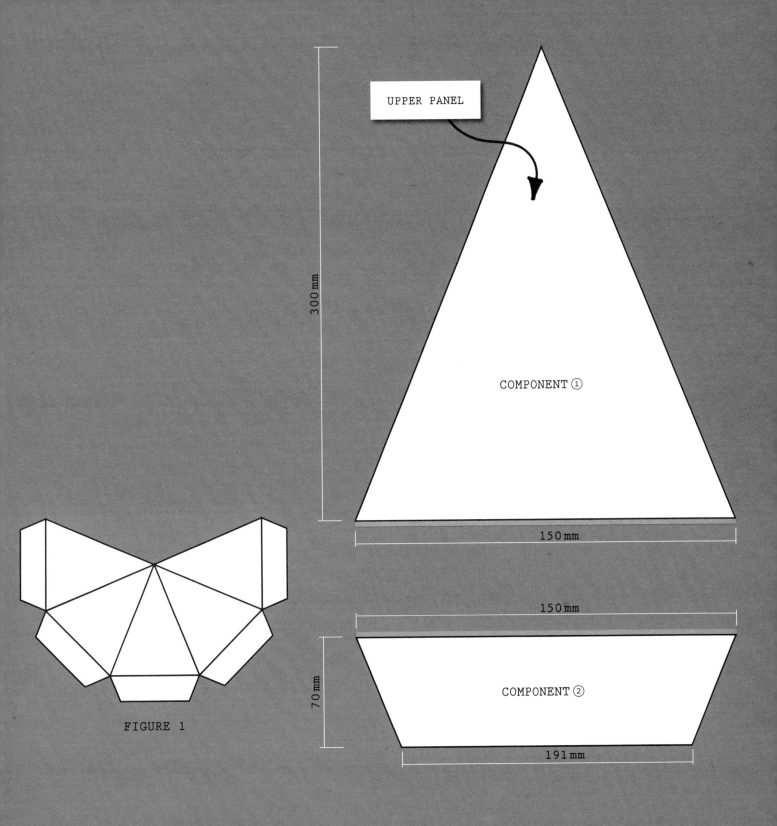

UPPER PANEL

COMPONENT ①

300 mm

150 mm

150 mm

COMPONENT ②

70 mm

191 mm

FIGURE 1

SMALL DIAMOND LAMP

The small diamond lamp creates a bright, focused spot of light.

MATERIALS & TOOLS

- ☐ Corrugated cardboard (2.5mm)
- ☐ Standard-size light fixture
- ☐ Standard size light bulb (LED or energy saver)

- ☐ Craft knife
- ☐ Ruler
- ☐ Triangle Protractor
- ☐ Pencil
- ☐ Kraft tape

Diamond lamps are a girl's best friend!

Fit the light bulb at least 40 to 50mm above the lower edge of the shade to keep it from being too bright when you look at it from the side.

Construction:

1 Draw each component six times and cut them out.

2 Lay the parts out as shown in Figure 1, with the back side of the cardboard facing up and the connecting edges facing outward. Attach everything together with kraft tape.

3 Tape the two outer edges of component ① together.

4 Tape the pieces of component ② together.

5 Cover the flaps from the outside with kraft tape.

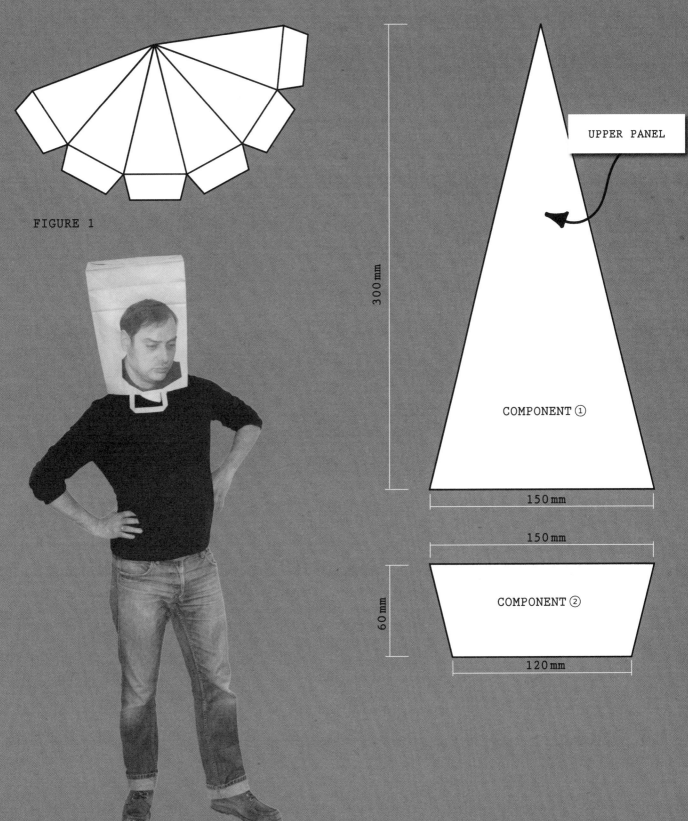

FIGURE 1

UPPER PANEL

300 mm

COMPONENT ①

150 mm

150 mm

60 mm

COMPONENT ②

120 mm

ACKNOWLEDGEMENTS   COPYRIGHT

It wouldn't be possible to create a book like "Cut, Fold & Hold" without help! You have to have people who inspire you with their crazy demands or wonderful ideas. You need people who are specialists in the areas that you yourself know nothing about. You need people who will visit you with food or a few beers, to bring you encouragement and urge you not to give up. You have to have those critically-minded people who want to check and double-check every project you come up with. And finally, the people who lend you the tools and ideas you didn't have but couldn't have progressed without. Yes, yes, yes, you need all of these people when you're putting a book together.

Therefore, we'd like to send our heartiest thanks to:
Anais, Antje, Cem, Corinna (the "Knipse!"), Marc, Markus, Paul, Ronny, Rüdiger, Sandra, Silke, Tom, Valentin, the brilliant Michael Fischer Edition publishing team, Rowland Hill (the inventor of the adhesive stamp), and all those well-known furniture stores that use beautiful cardboard boxes for their packaging!

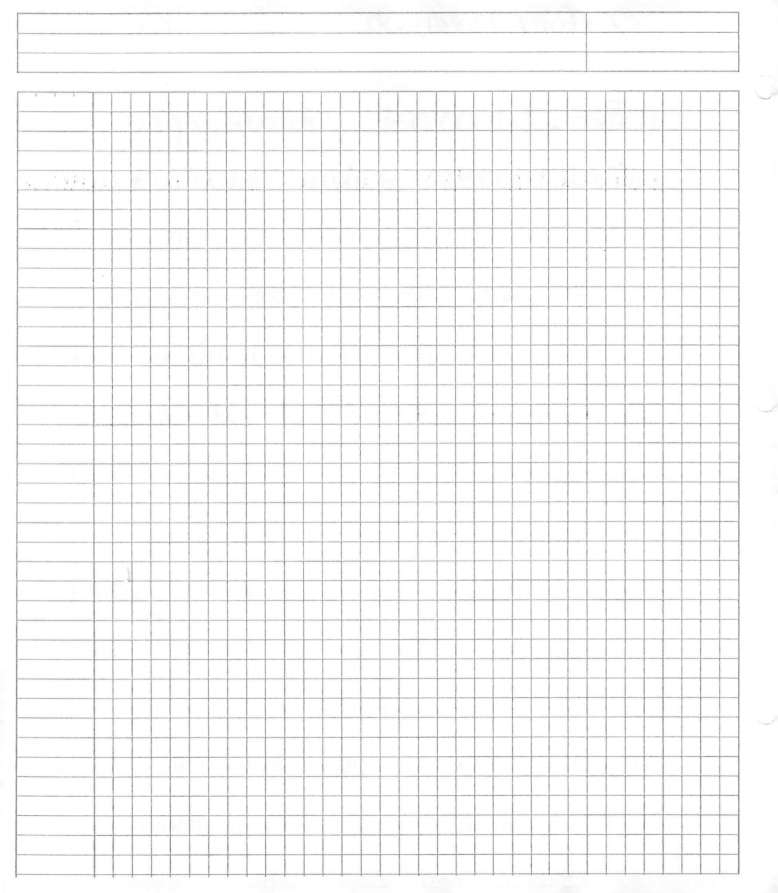